GABRIELLE BERKMAN-LEVINE

JESSICA BACAL is the director of the Wurtele Center for Work and Life at Smith College. Before coming to Smith, she taught elementary school in New York City. She holds an MS.Ed. from Bank Street College of Education and an MFA in creative writing from Hunter College, part of the City University of New York. She lives with her husband and two children in Northampton, Massachusetts.

Praise for *Mistakes I Made at Work*
Named by *Fast Company* as a "Top 10 Book You Need to Read This Year"
Named by *Publishers Weekly* as a "Top 10 Business/ Economics Book for Spring 2014"

"The printed equivalent of a long, hot bath at the end of a terrible day of work."   —*The New York Times*

"Refreshing . . . filled with humor and humiliation, plus loads of hard-earned career management advice." —*Elle*

"Absorbing . . . a comforting and genuine reminder that everyone makes mistakes." —*New York Magazine*

"Compelling . . . *Mistakes I Made At Work* shines in its recognition of the futility of the one-size-fits-all professional recommendation." —*Forbes*

"An important book . . . Crucial character boot camp for women everywhere." —*The Globe and Mail* (Toronto)

"Pure gold . . . [a] generous display of guts and wisdom." —*BUST*

"Remarkably refreshing . . . *Mistakes I Made At Work* will be of huge value to young women today who are working to find authentic passion, skills, and life goals amid layers of self-doubt, expectations, and high ideals." —verilymag.com

"An excellent book to give to a new grad, an old hand, an employee who's feeling red-faced, or YOU . . . You'll be glad you did." —*Houston Style Magazine*

MISTAKES I MADE AT WORK

25 Influential Women Reflect on What They Got Out of Getting It Wrong

EDITED BY JESSICA BACAL

A PLUME BOOK

PLUME
Published by the Penguin Group
Penguin Group (USA) LLC
375 Hudson Street
New York, New York 10014

USA | Canada | UK | Ireland | Australia | New Zealand | India | South Africa | China
penguin.com
A Penguin Random House Company

First published by Plume, a member of Penguin Group (USA) LLC, 2014

LIBRARY OF CONGRESS CATALOGING-IN-PUBLICATION DATA
Mistakes I made at work : 25 influential women reflect on what they got out of getting it wrong / edited by Jessica Bacal.
    pages   cm
  Includes bibliographical references and index.
  ISBN 978-0-14-218057-0
 1. Women—Vocational guidance.   2. Career development   3. Errors.
4. Experience.   5. Work—Psychological aspects.   I. Bacal, Jessica.
  HF5382.6.M57 2014
  650.1092'52—dc23
  2013045032

Printed in the United States of America
10

Set in Granjon

For Joe, Elijah, and Edie

Contents

INTRODUCTION

"**P**lease talk about a mistake you've made in your career and what you learned from it," said the panel moderator from the brightly lit stage. The audience of college students and professors emitted a low hum of anticipation.

I grabbed a pen, eager to hear what the five successful women sitting in front of me had to say. The topic was of personal interest to me, particularly given my recent change in career. It had been a risk for me to accept my role as inaugural director of Smith College's Wurtele Center for Work and Life, a challenge that I relished but that made me nervous. Although I wanted to do nothing wrong, chances to mess up were everywhere. Managing a budget, I overdelegated to a new assistant and ended up with a shortfall. Developing new leadership programs, I stepped on toes. I made errors on publicity materials, accidentally printing the wrong title for Julianna Smoot, who has held several high-level roles in the

Obama administration. Although she was gracious about it, I was mortified. For these and other blunders, I would spend days feeling like an imposter in my new role. Did others feel the same way? Did these women ever make such blunders?

Sitting in the panel audience with my notebook open, I wanted to hear something that would make me feel less alone, to fill a page with other people's stories. But after twenty minutes, that page was still blank—and oddly, this wasn't the first time I'd encountered such hesitation, or even avoidance, when it came to discussing errors on the job. For instance, my boss sent me to a leadership training week where several high-level women extolled the virtues of mistakes without talking about their own. Another time, I joined some students to hear from a notable visitor who generalized about her "sacrifices" and "trade-offs," never saying what they were.

To be fair, you could say these women were just putting their best foot forward and that it's difficult to talk about mistakes in a high-pressure situation. But over the years, I'd seen too many women waxing rhapsodic about "the value of learning from mistakes" without actually describing any, to find that platitude helpful. It was advice served, like mediocre breakfast pastries, at just about every professional conference. The average woman (like myself) hears it and thinks, "Sure, easy for *you* to say it's important to learn from mistakes, but your mistakes aren't like mine. Mine are *huge*." After all, if those who've "made it" ever *really* did anything wrong, they wouldn't be where they are now—right?

When I hear the imperative to "learn from your mistakes," I also hear echoes of the "good girl" messaging that permeates our culture. Starting in elementary school, girls feel "pressure to be perfect, accomplished, thin, and accommodating," according to a 2006 Girls Inc. report. This sounds exhausting—and it can also be damaging, keeping girls from stepping outside of their comfort zones. In 2007, psychologist Carol Dweck and her colleagues found that when learning new material, bright girls did not cope well with confusion. In fact, "the higher the girl's IQ, the worse she did." Girls were more likely than boys to become demoralized by a challenge, as if it called their ability into question. The pressure that those girls felt to "have it together" often follows young women to college and beyond. A well-known study at Duke University found that female students experienced a mandate of "effortless perfection." A 2013 *New York Times* article about Harvard Business School reported that women there participated in class less than men because—according to faculty and administrators—they "often felt they had to choose between academic and social success." It's as if even these high-powered go-getters didn't want to risk seeming too aggressive or giving a wrong answer. Clearly from girlhood through graduate school, we are absorbing unhelpful messages about the many ways in which we're supposed to do things "right"—and vague advice about "learning from mistakes" can blur unhelpfully into all of that.

But what if we heard stories about doing things wrong? I have witnessed the effects firsthand. After bestselling author

Rachel Simmons gave a speech at Smith College about dropping out of Oxford, students, transfixed, didn't want to leave
the hall. During a panel on failure, I saw looks of happy surprise come over students' faces when a faculty member talked
about a paper that hadn't been accepted in a prestigious journal. The young women I worked with expressed relief when
people they admired opened up about their own setbacks and
mistakes; in fact, they seemed to respect these people for feeling comfortable sharing narratives that weren't just "success
stories" but were instead laced with emotions like anxiety,
frustration, and shame.

As part of my job, I was reading up on leadership, discov-
ering what prominent experts believed leadership development actually looked like. Study after study showed that you
in fact *have to* learn from mistakes and keep going in order to
succeed. For example, psychologist Angela Duckworth's studies
of "grit"—the ability to persevere through errors and setbacks—
have led her to believe that it's one of the main ingredients in
achievement. The internationally known psychologist Daniel
Goleman writes about great leaders demonstrating "a thirst
for constructive criticism." Successful people are able to say to
themselves, "While I may have screwed up, it doesn't mean I
am a screwup." It was an insight that seemed provocative, and
it became the catalyst for this book.

I decided to interview interesting and influential women—
but instead of asking about all they'd done well, I'd ask about
what they *hadn't* done well. I'd collect stories to emphasize

what the research on leadership clearly showed but that many people just starting their careers often didn't understand: that making mistakes is part of growing at work.

While data show that high-achieving women *and* men feel pressure to be "perfect" in more or less equal measure, women may experience this pressure in unique ways, according to Patricia DiBartolo, a Smith College psychology professor who studies perfectionism. For example, women may feel social pressures more profoundly. Case in point—one day, five different people each e-mailed me a report from Princeton University that said that female students were less likely than male students to run for leadership positions, in part because of pressure to act in "socially acceptable" ways. *"This is not a Princeton-specific phenomenon,"* the report emphasized. Soon afterward, a nineteen-year-old Barnard College student named Julie Zeilinger published a piece on Forbes.com called "Why Millennial Women Do Not Want to Lead." "Young women today," she wrote, "are bred to doubt ourselves, question our worth and view ourselves as improvable projects rather than embrace the imperfection of our humanity." The article clearly hit a nerve: it received almost eighty thousand page views and was shared on Facebook almost ten thousand times.

It's important to understand, though, that the workplace casts a more critical eye on women. Researchers Alice Eagly and Linda Carli debunked the idea of a "glass ceiling," a barrier that exists only at the top. Instead, their extensive analyses show that gender bias in the United States is alive and well at entry-level *and* senior-level jobs, for blue-collar workers *and* executives. Women are more likely to get flack for mistakes, especially in typically "male" roles—this phenomenon is called "the glass cliff"—and studies show that women of color are *even more* at risk for being perceived as incompetent. If women are giving themselves tight margins for error, this could easily be seen as self-preservation. The problem is that anyone who wants to innovate, gain recognition, or become a leader will need to take risks and realize that mistakes are inevitable. While acknowledging that sexism still exists, each of us can also consider inhabiting the role of the "good enough leader"—one who screws up but stays in the game. And our cultural discourse on women's leadership must also create space for conversations about imperfection.

The women I interviewed were eager to break the silence. They understood the value of "mistake stories" as a kind of mentorship and agreed to contribute to this book even as our conversations disrupted their packed schedules: Luma Mufleh met me for breakfast between speeches about Fugees Family, her nonprofit devoted to child survivors of war; Cheryl Strayed was in the middle of an ongoing publicity tour for her bestselling memoir, *Wild*; legal scholar Lani Guinier fit in our conversations between filing a brief with the Supreme Court and turning in grades for her law students at Harvard.

As I collected the interviews, common themes began to emerge. Some women talked about walking away from terrible supervisors or from jobs that were sapping the life out of them;

this section is called "Learning to Say No." Other women discussed experiences that taught them self-advocacy; these are in "Learning to Ask." Stories in "Learning to Take Charge of Your Own Narrative" are about coming to recognize strengths and becoming more purposeful. And finally, there's a section called "Learning Resilience"—on getting back up after being knocked down.

Through listening to these lessons, and to the generous women who shared them, I've begun to tell my own stories. There's power in talking about our mistakes and failures. My hope is that in reading the stories in this book, you will be reminded that no one is perfect—not even these amazing women—and that it will help to propel you forward.

PART I

Learning to Take Charge of Your Own Narrative

After teaching elementary school and then freelancing to make money, I honestly couldn't believe my luck when I got a three-day-a-week job at Smith College on the Women's Narratives Project (WNP). And I was even more excited when I realized that it meant I sometimes got to sit around a table and talk with amazing women. WNP was the visionary brainchild of two deans, Maureen A. Mahoney and Jennifer L. Walters, who wanted students to reflect on and clarify their values and goals. In order to do this, they posed some seemingly illicit questions—illicit, anyway, in an environment of high achievers: What's the difference between what your family wants for you and what you want for yourself? What does success really mean to you? What would it be like to fail? Mahoney and Walters used the term "narratives" because it implies that the ways in which we understand and talk about ourselves are always evolving—it will likely be different in five or ten years than it is today. In addition, the word "narratives" alludes to multiplicity: "Each of us could tell several different stories about who we are right now," they reminded students.

I soon found that my own story was changing. This part-time "day job," one I'd initially accepted because I was a writer with a young child, was becoming something I cared about. I'd once thought that my career would feel gratifying *only* if I was publishing fiction, but I began to see this wasn't true because I loved talking to and working with college students. I'd once imagined that to be a good mother, I'd need to work a reduced schedule so that my son wouldn't have to be in "too much" child care. Now I was soaking up new research on women, work, and life, including a groundbreaking study that tracked one thousand infants over twenty years and showed that forty hours a week of quality child care doesn't interfere with development. (One of its principal investigators, Kathleen McCartney, later became Smith's president.) My son, I realized, was thriving at his loving preschool—even if I worked full-time, he'd be just fine. A new narrative was forming.

The ability to reflect on our own narratives is important for several reasons. It can help us to find a next step: in this section, Lani Guinier discusses coming to see that climbing the ladder from law clerk to lawyer to judge just wasn't for her and that she was happy to leave a prestigious job as a "referee" to work at the less prestigious, but more rewarding, NAACP Legal Defense and Educational Fund. Reflecting on our own narratives can also help us to advocate for ourselves in difficult situations: Reshma Saujani talks about the importance of becoming comfortable with sharing the fact that she'd taken out heavy loans for graduate school; this comfort allowed her to frame and share the story of her career leading up to a run for political office. Finally, understanding our own narratives can help us to make choices every day: Cheryl Strayed talks about the "paralyzing" nature of a writing task that just felt wrong, and the realization that she would need to be engaged in an authentic way with any assignment.

Even if we never put pen to paper (or fingers to keyboard), we are continually writing and rewriting our own life narratives. They help us to understand who we are now and where we are going. And they are always evolving.

LAUREL TOUBY

"I rejected the very idea of office politics. I felt it
was a waste of time. It just pissed me off. Why do I
need to go over there to get to here? It's like, Here's
what I want. Here's what you want. Let's get this
done."

"Don't be nervous" is what Laurel Touby says when we sit
down in a Manhattan Starbucks and she hears that
she's my first interview for this book. She checks that my tape
recorder is on; she moves it toward her to pick up her voice and
leans in close. In photos, you'll often see Laurel Touby in the
bright feather boa that she used to wear at her famous parties.
She is striking looking, and when she speaks publicly, she's
direct in a way that can be disarming. I'd anticipated feeling
intimidated by sitting down with her, but that's not the way it
actually felt at all. There's a generosity about Touby, an openness that put me completely at ease.

Laurel Touby founded the most successful networking site
for people in the publishing industry. It's called Mediabistro.com
and includes an incredible trove of information, including in-
structions on how to "pitch" to specific print and online magazines, courses that you can take online, job listings, and much

more. It all began in 1994 with a party she and a friend threw in order to meet other people in journalism and to feel less isolated in their lives as freelancers working from home. The parties became increasingly popular and spawned an e-mail newsletter (this was back in the early days of e-mail usage) and later a website—which became Mediabistro.com. In 2007, Touby sold the site for $23 million, and she now spends her time supporting other entrepreneurial ventures in a variety of ways.

Lessons I've Learned

Some work environments are a better fit than others.

My grandfather paid for my education, and that was my big break. It enabled me to pursue a career of my choosing without having debt hanging over me. But he also told me that I had to do something lucrative. "Work for a company that's going to pay you well and take care of you," he said. That was the mentality back then: companies take care of you. And I bought into it.

After college, I moved to New York City, where I literally knew only one person. Without the support of family and friends, I was anxious all the time. Even when I landed a job as a media planner for Young & Rubicam (at the time, the largest ad agency in the world) I felt as if I was holding on to a rock wall, just hanging on for dear life—which made it all the more upsetting when I was nearly fired.

I thought I was doing quite well at work, picking everything up. I was staying late and coming in on weekends; I was accomplishing all that was required of me, and like many women, I thought "my job" was only my performance. What I didn't realize was that I was also being judged by how I came across socially, even during downtimes. At the watercooler or over lunch, I'd been acting fun, casual, speaking my mind, cracking jokes—I wasn't shying away from being my true, somewhat edgy and irreverent self.

After about a month, my supervisor called me into her office and gestured to the chair across from her desk. I sat down, thinking I was going to be commended for a job well done. Instead, her face grave, she said, "Laurel, we're going to have to put you 'on watch.'"

"What do you mean, 'on watch'?" I asked.

She replied that they had a system there for monitoring employee behavior. People on watch were not fired immediately, but they were given a warning, which gave them time to try to improve and allowed supervisors to continue to assess them.

This took me completely by surprise. My brain hung on one final-sounding word. "Fired?" I asked, tears rolling down my face. "Why?" I had been so proud of myself and was just blindsided by this news. "What is wrong with me that I didn't see this?" I wondered.

She went on to say that the conversation wasn't about my

work at all, but that several people had reported to her that I was "mean." I guffawed through my tears. "Mean?" I asked incredulously. "What did I say that was mean?" She repeated back to me a few of the "mean" statements I had made. I explained to her that those had been lame little jokes I blurted out while standing in line at the copier or fixing my lipstick at the mirror in the bathroom. Having never experienced a professional environment, I was awkwardly trying to connect with my colleagues.

The consternation lifted from her face like a veil. She gave me a strange look and said, "You know, you don't *seem* mean. Look at you. Unless those are alligator tears, you seem very genuine and sweet. I think I know what's going on here. It could be a culture thing. Maybe you just don't fit in culturally and people don't understand your humor." But, I stammered, how could they not "understand" my humor? Isn't all humor pretty much the same? She pointed out that many of my colleagues were from the South or the Midwest. I was from an East Coast city— Miami, Florida. Perhaps my humor was a bit too ironic or cutting. "Why don't you stop making jokes," she suggested, "and let's meet again in a week's time?"

I had my doubts. I wondered how I could have been so off base in my very first job, when the stakes were so high. If I were fired, who else would hire me? I'd have to return to Miami to work for my grandfather's construction company. (He was actually eager for that, but to me it was the very definition of failure because it would mean I wasn't making it on my own.) Would I be able to switch off the joke making and present a "false face" to the world?

My supervisor opened up to me then. She explained that she understood all too well; in fact, she'd had to learn how to alter her personality when she began working for Y&R. "I've done it and you can do it, too," she said assuredly, explaining that she'd been the first black woman to be promoted from the secretarial pool to manager and then senior manager. "We're going to have to just prune you around the edges," she told me, with a bit too much glee. "You're a wild tree and we're going to make you into one of those well-manicured bushes." She was using the first two fingers on both hands to make scissoring motions high above her head, as if clipping away at a bush that had grown there.

"A topiary," I said. I'll never forget that image of her clipping my personality with her scissors—or my sudden realization that what she was *really* saying was that at the top of her game, she *still* couldn't be herself.

But I'm competitive and had to prove that I could fit in in corporate America. I stopped acting playful or making jokes, and I began to pay attention to every word that came out of my mouth, which meant I was straight and boring all the time. I had work "friends," but I tucked my real personality away when I was with them. Before the week was up, my supervisor called me in and told me that the watch had been lifted and that everything would be fine as long as I didn't joke anymore.

There's a set of corporate behaviors—ways of speaking, of addressing people, of responding to things—an entire protocol and vocabulary that I just forced myself to learn. While I eventually mastered these things, I began to wonder if working for a large, highly corporate entity might not be for me.

Even the best job is never a sure thing.

By the early 1990s, I decided that I had proven myself—I'd "done" corporate America. Looking for something more creative, I applied for a job at *Working Woman*, a magazine that was one of the first for women looking to build their careers. The editor in chief offered me the job, warning that I'd have to take a huge pay cut, but I was willing to do anything to escape my situation, including watching my salary drop from a meager twenty-two thousand dollars to an even more paltry sixteen thousand. Without hesitation I accepted, overjoyed to be working for a magazine I respected.

From the moment I stepped foot in the office, I felt like I was home. The place was all about nurturing its employees so that they could grow. "I could be here forever," I thought. My bosses were supportive and allowed me to take on increasingly ambitious projects, but at the same time there was a feeling of "put in your dues and wait, and you'll be rewarded." So I did. At first, I wrote the captions beneath photos, and then they let me write content for the little boxes that accompanied stories, then the sidebars, and finally, an actual article. I learned to edit and write headlines over the first three years that I worked there, and I was promoted and then promoted again, reaping the rewards of my hard work.

But then a new boss came in, and instead of kowtowing to her, I stayed loyal to the leader who had been pushed out—meaning, I didn't play politics.

We all had to apply for our jobs again, which included answering a survey so the new editor in chief could get to know us. One of the questions was "What are your favorite magazines?" A colleague told me, "I'm going to write that *Vanity Fair* is my favorite mag. I've read up on this editor, and I know she admires it." I thought this was ridiculous, since *Working Woman* was about women and their careers, and much of *Vanity Fair* is about pop culture and fashion and celebrities. I understood that the new editor in chief supposedly wanted to make *Working Woman* sexier, but I didn't agree with that. I read *Inc.* magazine, which is aimed at growing companies and is about the best ways to do business, and I thought our magazine should aspire to be like that. I went with my gut almost as an act of defiance—a show of loyalty to the previous editor. Somehow I hadn't remembered the lesson from my first job, which is that it's not always wise to place your personal authenticity ahead of the hive mind. To be honest, it's stupid if you want to survive in a big corporation.

Still, in my wildest dreams I didn't think I could get fired for expressing my opinion. I put stock in the virtue of hard work: if you had a high-performing employee, you kept her. But doing a good job—and essentially playing the role of a good girl—doesn't necessarily lead to security.

This was the experience that taught me that wherever you go, whatever job you take, you always want to be working on boosting your career skills, not in the hopes that you'll get a reward from your current company or boss—because they might not be there one day. Instead, you almost need to see yourself as a freelancer, building skills and capabilities to take with you to the next job and the next job and the next job. That's your toolkit, and you should be adding to it all the time, because you can't rely on a company to take care of you and nurture you and bring you up in the world the way they used to back in my grandfather's time.

I was horrified to learn that the new editor of *Working Woman* had intentions to wholesale fire half the staff. She didn't care about us and all that we had worked for. She didn't care about all that I had accomplished. It wasn't school, it was business, and she wanted her team in there. She left me a message at home saying, "Call me back." I was having knee surgery, and when I listened to my answering machine I was a little bit outraged—not only did she not realize that I was in the hospital, but she was planning to fire me over the phone!

I'd been at *Working Woman* for three years on the Monday that I hobbled into the office, pretending I'd never gotten the phone message. I was scared to go in there on my crutches and face her and the pain and fear. Still, I pushed myself to be strategic, and I sat down and negotiated a deal to write for the magazine, which I don't know if she would have been willing to give me over the phone. Then I was on the streets, but at least I had a contract.

Even in your own business, you still have to cope with office politics because you're managing people.

I began networking again. I had done a good job of staying in touch with connections in publishing, and a colleague at *Glam-*

our said that there was an opening for a business editor. I was hired to work from home, on contract, turning in assignments once a month. Now there was no chance of my going into an office, being myself, and shaking things up!

During those years of working without colleagues, I began hosting cocktail parties because I was lonely and wanted to meet people. I micromanaged the parties, making sure everything was right. The music couldn't be too loud; the space couldn't be too dark. I forced the guests to introduce themselves to each other, moving them around in the room. Some would get annoyed, and others would relax and just go with it.

People were just starting to use e-mail at that time, and I began e-mailing the guests to invite them. When I decided to launch a website, the Internet felt pretty much brand-new. The site was going to be a way for people who went to the parties to learn about job openings and to connect online. I soon found that I was good at coming up with a vision to make it grow. For example, we began saying to people who posted jobs that they should send us one hundred dollars if it was helping them find employees. If it wasn't, then they shouldn't send anything. Thousands of dollars' worth of checks started coming in. We also offered online classes for people in publishing, which became popular and made a lot of money. In 2000, I was able to raise a slug of capital, five hundred thousand dollars, to expand the company.

With the cash, I began to assemble my own team. I hired six young people, just out of college. They were doing what I wanted—more or less—and I was top dog. One day, one of them came into my office. He knew me well, because he'd been my first intern. He said, "You're upsetting people and we're all ready to quit."

Holy shit, I thought. It was all happening again. I'm not fit for an office environment—even my own office!

He said, "When you are upset with someone—or about something—you can't show your anger and disappointment. You need to control yourself more."

I thought, "Great, I can't do anything." I felt like I shouldn't be around people: keep Laurel away from people! I apologized to everybody and admitted that I was learning how to be a manager. And after, I tried to be gentler. I worked on the phrasing of things, so instead of saying, "I don't think this is going to work; can you fix this, this, and this?" or "That press release needs to sound more alive," I would say, "This part is great, but let's fix that so it sounds more alive." Same message but sugarcoated.

We did have some people quit, but we had a core group of five who stayed with me from day one all the way to the moment we sold the company and even after the sale. Eventually the company became so successful that I was able to hire someone to manage my staff; I remained the outward-facing person who dealt with the press and with customers. And years later, those first employees came to me and said, "You really cared about my career development and about teaching me, even though at the time I didn't understand." That was gratifying.

To create a business, you have to be assertive. You have to be fast. You can't waste time. You don't *have* time, so you act first and worry about it later. In the corporate environment, risk is *not* encouraged. It's worry first, and maybe act later, maybe not . . . maybe never get there. Being an entrepreneur, implementing my own vision and subsequently working with other small businesses to help implement theirs, is much better suited to my personality than being employed by a big company. Even though my grandfather thought that a long-term job would offer me security, he couldn't imagine how the world would evolve—because companies just don't provide that to people anymore. That's why it's important these days to build the capacity to contribute within your field and also to pursue work environments that feel like the right fit for you.

LAUREL TOUBY'S TIPS

▶ Wherever you go, whatever job you take, you always want to be working on skills you can take with you. For example, learning HTML or the newest Windows operating system; taking courses or doing extra reading about your industry—anything to help you build your "toolkit."

▶ Know yourself, and don't try to be someone you're not. Don't try to shove down your personality if you have too much personality for the corporate environment.

RACHEL SIMMONS

"The college application industrial complex puts you on a ruthless treadmill of racking up accomplishments to bolster a college application. The danger of the treadmill is that you can end up training for someone else's race instead of pursuing the life that will be fulfilling to you."

When college students are asked about what it's like to work with bestselling author and leadership consultant Rachel Simmons, they use words like "approachable," "funny," "helpful," "refreshingly honest," and "relatable" to describe her personality. One student said, "I honestly believe that if all girls and young women were exposed to her workshops, it would change the world." Simmons has spent the last several years working with undergraduates at schools like Smith, Barnard, and Simmons. Her workshops, which students love, are opportunities to have fun while learning self-awareness and setting goals for clear communication and risk taking.

Simmons came to this work after first parsing the language of female aggression in her bestseller *Odd Girl Out*. Based on three hundred interviews at ten different schools, the book catalyzed a new cultural conversation about girls' relationships and development. It was originally published in 2002; in a recently updated and expanded edition, Simmons explores the ways in which aggression can play out online and offers concrete advice for parents, teachers, and girls themselves. Reviewing the updated edition for *Slate*, writer Jordan Kisner said, "*Odd Girl Out* is gripping because it's relatable, even to those of us who are mercifully removed from the social politics of middle and high school. By documenting girls' social lives with depth and nuance (no girl is *just* a bully or *just* a victim, Simmons reminds us) the book encourages us to consider what transpired at our own lunch tables, and how that shaped the kind of women we became."

Simmons's follow-up, *The Curse of the Good Girl*, is also a must-read for any young woman who has ever felt pressure to be nice, polite, modest, or selfless. Many of the themes in these books are explored in Simmons's current work with undergraduate women.

Lessons I've Learned

Life is not a game that you always need to be winning.

I was a late bloomer. I didn't become "good at school" until I went to college at Vassar, where I suddenly felt like I could spread my wings. My grades were outstanding. I took leadership positions at the college: editor of the weekly newspaper, student assistant to the president. I worked hard and I played hard. I came out as a gay. It was an idyllic four years.

After I graduated, my accomplishments continued to pile up. I was an Urban Fellow in the Mayor's Office in New York. I advanced quickly and within a year was presiding over meetings in the basement of city hall. In my next job, I was recruited to work on a Senate campaign that became the most watched political event in the country. I accompanied my candidate to various events, meeting then president Clinton and a bunch of celebrities. In the blink of an eye, I was climbing the ladder in Manhattan's political universe. I loved the exposure to power, the attention, the status. I decided to go to law school, a common "next step" when you're getting into politics; I applied and was accepted at Yale.

At about this time, the Career Development person at Vassar approached me about applying for the Rhodes scholarship. I balked at first—I loved my life in New York—but I never turned down an opportunity to win, so I applied. The whole application process became a game. I would put my mind to this, and I would accomplish it, just as I'd done with everything else.

Mayor Giuliani held a press conference in the Blue Room at city hall to celebrate my selection as a Rhodes scholar. The *Daily News* ran a headline on page two: "Finally, a Genius in City Hall." Vassar photographed me for their admissions literature, and off I went to the University of Oxford, in England, deferring law school for the moment.

My plan was to be the best Rhodes scholar ever. I would put my mind to it, and accomplish it, because that was what I always did.

Don't privilege how you appear to others over how you feel inside.

When I sat down at my desk at Lincoln College, and looked out the window at the rainy courtyard, I knew something was wrong. I tried my best to ignore the feeling, but it persisted. I went out with the other Rhodes scholars. I went to political theory class. I did my homework. But instead of enjoying these things, I was plagued by questions.

Why were the other Rhodes scholars so obsessed with their public images and their futures?

Why were all our seminar readings written before 1965?

Why did one of my tutors snicker when I brought up feminist political theory?

Why were people putting mayonnaise on hard-boiled eggs?

And why was it getting dark at three thirty in the afternoon?

I was trying my best to put my mind to the task at hand, but I couldn't truly engage with what I was supposed to be doing, and so I couldn't get my work done.

It was the first time in my life this had ever happened to me, and I couldn't handle it. I was hitting a wall and slowly sank into a depression.

I wandered the foggy streets of Oxford feeling lost. I wanted desperately to go home, but how could I quit? How could I walk away from this, one of the greatest accomplishments for a young American? Who did that? It would be totally humiliating. And I was no quitter. So I kept pushing myself. I would do it. I would accomplish this.

In the meantime, I spent weeks reading, walking, going on runs, and, truth be told, crying. I kept thinking, Who am I? How did I get here? How did I wind up in a country I didn't particularly care to be in, with people so unlike me, reading books that put me to sleep?

The answer was that I had become a Rhodes scholar not because I wanted to study at Oxford for two years, but because I wanted the recognition. Winning awards, after all, was what I did. My self-esteem, the basic foundation of who I was, had been built on it. When I could not win for the first time in my life—when I could not set my mind to going after something and accomplishing it—I fell apart.

What did I really care about? What did I really feel passion for? I had been jumping through hoops for so long, doing what I thought I was supposed to do, that I forgot why I was doing any of it in the first place. I forgot what I was striving for. I had lost myself.

I decided that if I was to change the situation, I had to figure out who I was again. I had to know what I really cared about—just because I cared about it, and not because anyone wanted me to, or because it would win me awards.

I went to the library at Oxford. There was no assignment, no mandate, no honor to be won. I started thinking about an experience I had had at the age of eight, when a girl named Abby made my best friends run away from me on the playground, leaving me painfully alone, just as I was now. Why did it bug me so much? Why had it stayed in my mind? At the time, no one had studied the topic of girls' aggression, so I started to. I pursued something I was interested in, just because I cared about it.

Somewhere along the way, I got it into my head to write a children's book. Bullied girls would know they were not alone, that this terrible experience would not last forever, nor would it define them. At the same time, I finally realized that I had to leave Oxford. I packed my bags and moved out of my flat. I knew I didn't belong there and I had to accept that I had made a mistake. If others judged me, so be it.

My family was deeply disappointed in me. My father, who had in his life not achieved what I had, begged me to reconsider. How could I walk away from such an opportunity? How could I be so ungrateful?

I moved in with my parents, and my resolve about leaving Oxford began to fade. I felt embarrassed and ashamed. I felt like I was a quitter after all. A high-ranking official at Vassar said I had embarrassed the college. It was a very sad time for me.

One day, I e-mailed a friend whose mother was a book editor and gave her a summary of my children's book idea.

Eventually, she replied that it was not the right idea, but she would have lunch with me. My father said, "Well, you didn't think you'd get a positive reply from the very first editor you contacted, did you?"

I almost didn't call her. After all, she didn't like my idea very much. But as I sat on the floor of my childhood bedroom, looking at a cabinet full of dusty trophies, I figured, What do I have to lose?

When I reached Jane, the editor, she told me about her fortieth high school reunion, when she saw the girl who had once been mean to her. She had never forgotten the experience. "You're on to something with this book idea of yours," she told me, "but you can't write a children's book. You have to write the book." She asked me if I had heard of *Reviving Ophelia*, and of course I had; it was a bestseller about teenaged girls that had sold over a million copies. Jane had edited it.

And this was how my first book was born. Jane mentored me through the entire process. I received a small advance. I withdrew from law school. This time, my parents were furious. My father shouted at me: "You're throwing away every opportunity you've been given."

I didn't care. If I wanted to reapply to law school, I would. I suspected this book would heal me and bring me back to myself. To earn extra money, I became a nanny in Manhattan. I took short-term, menial jobs. I moved to a mouse-infested apartment in Brooklyn. But I knew what I felt most committed to in the world, and I was doing it.

It seemed incredible: of the hundreds, maybe thousands, of editors in the world, I had found the one who'd edited *Reviving Ophelia*, entirely by fate. But was it fate or was it passion? I am not a believer in predestination, but I do think that on some level, my passion led me to Jane. When I devoted myself to what I genuinely cared about, when I let my heart guide me (as opposed to my need to accomplish) I found true success.

A week after *Odd Girl Out* was published, I was on *Oprah*. The book spent three months at the top of the *New York Times* bestseller list. These hoops were wonderful, but they weren't the point. I'd learned that when you privilege how you appear to others over how you are to yourself—when you choose seeming over being—you drift away from the strongest parts of who you are. The right to claim personal authority in your life is about claiming passion, and passion is what feeds our most important convictions and values.

RACHEL SIMMONS'S TIPS

▶ Listen to your "internal voice," that voice inside your head that tells you when you feel tired or thirsty, whether you should leave that party, if you should buy that cool shirt. When you think about the path you're on right now, what does the voice say? A full-throated, passionate *yes*? A maybe? Or an I-hate-this-but-it's-what-I-have-to-do? You can plug your ears for a while, but eventually, that voice grows louder, more ominous, and harder to ignore. Listen to it now before you get in too deep.

▶ Don't be afraid to quit. Who cares what other people think? They're not the ones living your life. You are. The people we are terrified of disappointing usually want us to be happy. Take the leap and trust that you will land on the other side.

▶ There is no school, no therapy session, no amount of money that will earn you the wisdom and strength conferred by an epic-fail mistake. It's like when babies touch something hot and scream in pain. They'll never touch it again. And neither will you.

CORINNA LATHAN

"Starting a company and leaving academia, I had so many friends, male and female, who were just terrified for me—terrified that it wouldn't work out and then I'd be both humiliated *and* out of a job. But I didn't feel that way, because I wasn't afraid of failing. Part of that confidence was being able to ask, 'What's the worst that could happen?' The answer was that I could probably go back to academia (with my tail between my legs) or find something else interesting to do!"

D r. Cori Lathan has the coolest job ever: she works with robots. As founder and CEO of the engineering research and design firm AnthroTronix, Lathan leads a team of engineers to come up with amazing inventions aimed at helping all kinds of people, from military personnel to children with cerebral palsy. For example, they created a glove that allows soldiers on night patrol to communicate by silently moving their hands. They also built an interactive little guy, called Cosmo-Bot, whose purpose is to make physical therapy fun for kids.

Lathan's work has been featured in *Forbes*, *Time*, and the *New Yorker* and has earned her recognition as Maryland's "Top Innovator of the Year," as one of *MIT Technology Review*'s

"Top 100 World Innovators," and as one of *Fast Company*'s "Most Creative People in Business."

Because her family always supported her love of math and science, Lathan now works to make sure that other girls get the same kind of encouragement. She's the founder of a program for junior high school girls called Keys to Empowering Youth, an adviser for two different robotics programs for kids, and a member of the board of Engineering World Health.

Lathan received her BA in biopsychology and mathematics from Swarthmore College; at MIT she earned a master's degree in aeronautics and astronautics and a PhD in neuroscience.

Lessons I've Learned

Even if you do advanced study within an academic field, it doesn't mean you have to go into academia.

As a kid, I loved *Star Trek* and I wanted to be an astronaut so I could explore space like they did on the show. I was good in school, and my parents' encouragement gave me the confidence to pursue courses in the STEM fields (science, technology, engineering, math), where I was often one of the only girls in class. There are several reasons that fewer girls enter these fields—including the extremely boring state of math and science education in the United States and the media glamor-ization of other pursuits, like acting and singing and playing sports. In addition, parents and teachers often don't recognize their own gender biases and so unwittingly fail to encourage girls in STEM fields even if they don't actively *discourage* them. I, on the other hand, had so much support and confidence that even though I failed out of engineering my freshman year of college, I went on to receive an engineering degree from MIT!

The only problem was that after I succeeded in getting that degree, I made the mistake of going into academia. I'd always known that I wanted to get my PhD and thought that meant I had to be a professor; I really didn't consider other options. However, after being at MIT for six years as a student, I real-ized that the publish-or-perish pressure of a "Research I" uni-versity was not for me and that I wanted a balance of teaching and research and service. So when I graduated, I went to teach at a good second-tier university with a strong undergraduate population—and what I discovered was that academia is aca-demia. It felt like a cult with this bizarre attitude that if you are there, you must want tenure and you're going to do anything to get it.

Young faculty get taken advantage of because they "can't" say no: They have to teach courses that senior faculty don't want, during the worst time slots. They have to teach *new* courses, which require a lot of prep and are a huge drain. (In my first two years, I taught eight.) Since I was the only woman in the school of engineering, I was asked to be on practically every committee, which would have been fine if I'd gotten "credit" for it, but when I went up for tenure, I had professors asking, "Why don't you have more publications?"—and it seemed like they meant, "What have you been *doing* with your time?"

What really made me leave, though, was *not* a lack of promotions or tenure—they ultimately tried to give me both. It was the lack of accountability in the research we were doing. I was supposed to be satisfied with just writing papers on how robots could help kids with disabilities achieve basic, everyday tasks, and I thought, "My God, there's a market there. There's a need for this technology. How can I do research on these kids and look the parents in the eye when they ask, 'So how can I get a robot like the one we've been testing to make my kid's physical therapy fun?' How can I tell them, 'There isn't one'?"

As I came to this realization, an amazing thing happened: A business incubator—a whole building for new companies— went up across the street from where I was teaching. I'd never thought of myself as an entrepreneur but I walked in and said, "What do I have to do to apply?"

I worked with two of my students to write a business plan for a company that would create the kind of robot we'd been testing and writing about in our academic work. I approached it just like any other grant proposal: They give you an outline and you fill it in—what's the product, what's the market? You act like you're sure about everything, even when you're not. The incubator loved the idea and let us in with the caveat that we needed to find a business person to guide us, which we did. I took a leave of absence from the university and had so much fun that year I never went back.

Failure is part of innovation.

Our company is interested in questions about humans' interface with technology. With the University of Maryland's Human-Computer Interaction Lab, we codeveloped a storytelling robot named CosmoBot that kids could interact with through wearable sensors. A child doing physical therapy who needed to practice raising her arm, for example, could suddenly make CosmoBot raise *his* arm at the same time, which was motivating! A child with autism who needed to practice interactive speech could get CosmoBot to respond in a game that was also a back-and-forth dialogue.

We were able to build the robot and test it in schools, but at that point we realized, "Holy cow, we've just spent $750,000 in grant funding to build *one* robot, and all we have is a prototype with a couple of data points—to get this to manufacturing is going to be insanely expensive." Even after we raised a million more dollars and the National Science Foundation matched it, we realized there was no way we could launch this product.

Given the consumer electronics revolution (in short: everyone has smartphones) we thought that developing an interactive robot for kids should be within our grasp—but we were totally wrong for a lot of reasons. The biggest one is that making hardware is, well, hard. It's technically difficult and extremely expensive to build an actual object, because each iteration is a whole new manufacturing process. From a business perspective, our product was also a disruptive technology, which means it's designed to change the way that people do business, and so by definition is "wrong" for the current market. Some people are able to create markets out of nothing; in our case, we weren't.

However, we had built this thing called Mission Control, which was—still is—a fantastic interface. It was a special kind of keyboard that went with our robot, and it had these big, round, colorful buttons that were like dimmer switches, making it a much more physical interface than a regular keyboard. Kids seemed to feel comfortable using it. We decided to build a learning system around it and assembled a team of experts to write compatible educational software. The whole thing became what we called Cosmo's Learning System. It ended up being our flagship product, and everyone loved it, and we sold a bunch to various school systems. It has since been used with able-bodied kids, kids with autism, and kids with cerebral palsy, and it really put us out there as soup-to-nuts product developers and innovators.

In my original field of academic research, you develop a hypothesis and if you can't prove it, you don't call it "a mistake" or "being wrong." You say, "I was unable to disprove the null hypothesis." And in the world of entrepreneurs, people wear their mistakes like badges of honor; you'll hear them say things like, "I had three failed companies before I had my success," or "Venture capital doesn't want to fund a new entrepreneur, because he or she hasn't made some mistakes." We all understand that mistakes are part of the process of innovation.

This is why I think the STEM fields and the entrepreneurial world actually provide great environments for women—who are often hard on themselves—because they allow you to accept mistakes and keep going. If we could convince young women to go into STEM fields purely for that reason, wouldn't it be great?

CORINNA LATHAN'S TIPS

▶ I think taking risks can be hard for women, but it helps to have a "what's the worst that can happen?" attitude. I knew that if my company failed, I'd be able to move on. I had credentials that no one could take away and the resilience to not internalize failure—it didn't have to define me.

▶ Even though we've had several products that were market failures, they helped people to get to know who we are, and we leveraged that visibility to get other contracts and work on new products. So we see "failure" as just part of doing our work, part of innovation. I think that we all might be able to value our mess-ups and mistakes a little more if we saw them as part of the process of developing as people.

▶ In any field, our resilience is tested. Sometimes it's a sign that it's time to move on—like when I left academia—and sometimes it's just a bump on the road to achieving your dreams. Discerning the difference is the challenge and there is not one right answer!

LANI GUINIER

"When I, a young girl watching television, saw Constance Baker Motley escort James Meredith to the University of Mississippi at Oxford, it had a profound effect on me. She was physically very powerful—both determined and serious. And the fact that it was a woman who was playing this significant role in the desegregation of Old Miss—that's what I focused on: that a woman could be a lawyer—and a brave lawyer."

In 1998, Lani Guinier, Harvard's Bennett Boskey Professor of Law, was the first female African American professor to receive tenure at Harvard Law School. Before teaching at Harvard, she served as a special assistant in the Civil Rights Division of the U.S. Department of Justice under President Carter, then worked as a lawyer for the NAACP Legal Defense and Educational Fund. In 1993, she was nominated by then president Bill Clinton, an old friend and Yale Law School classmate, to return to the Department of Justice and lead its Civil Rights Division. She quickly came under attack from conservatives for her writings on voting and democracy, and President Clinton withdrew the nomination. Guinier responded with grace and resilience; instead of retreating, she seized the opportunity to begin promoting public discourse about the intersection of race, gender, and the law. She published several books on these topics, including a memoir about that time called *Lift Every Voice: Turning a Civil Rights Setback into a New Vision of Social Justice.*

Guinier grew up in New York City, where her mother was a public school teacher and her father worked and attended law school at the same time. She remembers him having to take a bus and then two subways to travel from St. Albans, Queens, to New York University Law School in Manhattan. "He loved law school," Guinier says, "and the other person who loves it is my son. But I enjoyed being a lawyer more than I enjoyed being a law student." Part of her feeling about law school likely has to do with the story that she tells below.

Lessons I've Learned

Sometimes it takes the wrong job to realize what's a good fit for you.

In 1971 I went to law school at Yale, determined to become a civil rights lawyer. The year before I arrived, there had been a lot of turmoil in New Haven because the Black Panthers were on trial there. Protests on campus and in the city had led to an atmosphere of agitation in the law school; I think some teachers began to associate the black students with militancy and felt threatened, which compounded the outrage that black students had at feeling they did not belong. For whatever reason, Yale admitted far fewer black students during my year than they had in the year prior: I was one of twelve in a class of two hundred. But I had a strong support network of black peers from college, and there was a tremendous sense of solidarity among us.

In my second year, I took a course called Business Units One. It was taught by a professor who would come into class every day and say, "Good morning, gentlemen." He acknowledged on the first day that there were some women in the class, but he said that we, too, would become "gentlemen of the bar." I actually felt much more excluded from the law school as a result of that interaction than from everything that was happening in New Haven with regard to black student demonstrations or ongoing civil and criminal cases in New Haven. The women's movement was at a very early stage, and to be told that in order to be a lawyer, I had to become a "gentleman" . . . I didn't have anybody to talk to about that. I could make a joke of it, but it wasn't as if there was the same kind of activism or awareness regarding women's issues as there was about race, compared to even ten years later. Instead, there was a sense of not being present in the room even as you were sitting right there.

After graduating from law school, I accepted a clerkship with Judge Damon Keith, who had been one of the very first black lawyers to be elevated to a federal court judgeship in Detroit. There was an atmospheric difference between Detroit and New York City, where I'd grown up. Detroit was so friendly that at first it frightened me; I was unaccustomed to speaking to strangers, because in New York City everyone is rushing and you barely have time to speak to anyone, even people you *know*. In Detroit, by contrast, people would come up to Judge Keith, say hello, and start a conversation. Most—but not all—of the people greeting him were black, but regardless of whoever stopped to say hello, that person almost always projected a sense of camaraderie and admiration toward him. Even if he was in a hurry, he would stop and at least have a short conversation. This was something he kept tutoring me on: "If somebody says hello, you must say hello back. And if they say your name, that's a reason to continue the conversation, even if you can't remember their name."

I came to love Detroit's warmth, and the sense of belonging to a community, so I stayed there even after my clerkship was over, taking a job as a referee in the Wayne County Juvenile Court, where I sat in judgment on criminal cases (but not serious felonies) and on cases of neglect and abuse. It was great on paper because it came with money and a step up in title—but I didn't like it.

Having worked with a federal judge, I wanted to learn about the state courts and the juvenile justice system, but what I learned was not affirming. The juvenile court felt like a neglected part of the city and the community. It was full of many sad and sometimes strange stories: a couple wanted to be released from their obligation to adopt a child; a social worker wanted to take a child from the mother because there were no curtains on the living room windows. Each day I was summoned at eight in the morning and given eight cases, and I couldn't go to lunch until after I was finished with all of them.

When setting bail, I sat in a closet-sized room right beside the police officers, the juvenile, and sometimes the parents. I knew I didn't have the best information because the defense lawyers and social workers weren't able to do thorough investigations, and yet I was often prodded by the officers to set bail so high that the kid would have to stay in detention. I'd been taught in law school that bail is set so that the accused shows up, and if the juvenile did show up to this part of the process, especially with his or her parents, I would feel confident that yes, the juvenile would return, and then I would set an appropriate bail. Yet there was often this unspoken sense that if you didn't send this child to detention, the police officers—who were really your colleagues—would stop being collegial. There was this pressure to shift my own views, and I didn't like the effect of it. Working in the legal system in this way was like expecting to hear a symphony only to find it was being played by a lone harmonica player; it was jarring and dissatisfying.

Needless to say, I didn't thrive in the work. It didn't build on my strengths, and it also made me feel vulnerable: At the supermarket, a teenage boy or girl might shout out, "Hello,

Referee Guinier," and I'd be second-guessing—how does this person know me? What did I do to him or her? There was a sense of not being able to leave my job even after I went home.

But my mother was always of the opinion that mistakes are learning opportunities, and the takeaway lesson for me was that I never wanted to be a judge. This was a great revelation, because in order to be esteemed in the legal profession, you are supposed to be aspiring to be a judge. I didn't want to be sitting in judgment, I realized, when I wasn't in a position to go out and interview witnesses to amass the facts myself but instead would have to make decisions based on potentially unreliable information. I didn't like that at all, and understanding that part of myself was key.

Being part of a high-functioning team can make all the difference at work.

The job I had wanted all my life was to be a civil rights lawyer like Constance Baker Motley. When I was offered a position working with Assistant Attorney General Drew S. Days at the Civil Rights Division of the Department of Justice, I left Detroit and moved to Washington, DC, for that job. In 1980, after Ronald Reagan was elected president, Mr. Days left to join the faculty at Yale Law School. I, too, was lucky: I got my dream job with the NAACP Legal Defense and Educational Fund (LDF), the same place Constance Baker Motley had worked when I, as a child, had seen her on television. The Voting Rights Act of 1965 (the VRA) was set to expire in 1982, and although I hadn't thought that legislative advocacy was what I'd do, it ended up that I loved working on amending and extending the VRA. I felt privileged to be part of a legislative team: it was exciting to be among a group of lawyers, activists, and members of Congress who were influencing history. After the VRA was renewed, I found myself ensconced in New York City working at LDF. I was thrilled to actually hold the same job that my childhood role model had had—I was now a civil rights litigator.

There was something very special about working at LDF. When I opened the door in the morning and crossed the threshold to enter the offices, I knew everyone there was on my side. I could go to anybody's office and say, "I have this really difficult case," and they'd stop what they were doing and talk through it with me. The opportunity to collaborate—and the valuable lessons that I learned from my peers—taught me that there was no way you could take on these battles by yourself and there were a lot of ways to fail.

I realized that for me, collegiality and emotional connection were like an energy supplement. At the juvenile court there had been no team; everyone was in his or her own courtroom; as a referee, you sat in judgment on other people's lives but couldn't consult with anyone because you had eight cases before lunch. Plus, as a referee, I was prohibited from interviewing witnesses or leaving my chambers. I was not allowed

to be a detective. I was not equipped, in other words, to un-
cover the real story. And even though *that* job (at least for some
people) had more status and paid more than my work at LDF,
it wasn't restorative. In contrast, there was an exuberance that
came from working at LDF. It's what you might imagine a
football or basketball team experiences when they're hot: pass-
ing the ball to each other, with no one person acting like a
prima donna, because they're coordinating to achieve a commonly shared goal—to succeed as a team.

To me, the story of my early career is really about libera-
tion. It's liberating to free yourself from the assumption that
the best way to succeed is to keep moving up a ladder, where
you become more and more "important" and more and more
powerful. If you have to subdue or disregard your values, if
you have to forgo your intellectual interests and lack the necessary evidence to be truly fair and just, then becoming important and powerful is just not worth it.

LANI GUINIER'S TIPS

▶ My mother told me that even though I was very comfortable in Detroit, I was "too young to be middle-
   aged" and should go to Washington, DC, to take a
   job I was being offered with the Civil Rights Division
   at the Department of Justice. She would remind me:
   "You can always go back to Detroit if that turns out to
   be what you want." Sometimes being comfortable in

a place isn't a good enough reason to stay there. It's okay to take risks.

▶ Money and a high-status job title aren't everything when they fail to produce a sense of genuine satisfaction at work.

▶ When I'm teaching, I often share with my students this quote from Howard Thurman, a theologian who greatly influenced Dr. Martin Luther King Jr.: "Don't just ask what the world needs. Ask what makes you come alive, and go do it. Because what the world needs is people who have come alive."

ILEANA JIMÉNEZ

"I said to myself, 'Before I'm thirty, I'm going to do three things: move home to New York; find a school that matches my vision and mission; and come out to my family and at work.' Once I did all those things, I catapulted myself into a much more empowering time in my career."

Students who are lucky enough to have Ileana Jiménez as their high school teacher can take classes in feminism, LGBT (lesbian, gay, bisexual, transgender) literature, Toni Morrison, and memoir writing. Jiménez teaches English at the Little Red School House and Elisabeth Irwin High School (LREI) in New York City, where she has also worked with her students to raise awareness about sexual harassment, sex trafficking, the sexualization of girls and women in the media, and queer youth issues. Jiménez's mission as a teacher is to use the "classroom itself as a space to engage in real discussions that will allow young people to transform not just themselves, but the world around them."

In recognition of her work teaching feminism and activism to high school students, the New York City chapter of the National Organization for Women gave her the Susan B. Anthony Award in 2012. In 2010, the Feminist Press named her one of its "40 Feminists Under 40."

Jiménez has written about education and feminist issues for publications such as *Feministing*, the *Huffington Post*, *Ms.* magazine, *On the Issues*, and the Women's Media Center. Her blog, *Feminist Teacher*, provides cutting-edge ideas for K–12 teachers who want to bring feminism and activism to their classrooms. Her creation of the Twitter hashtag #HSfeminism has united teachers in the conversation nationally and globally.

She received her MA in English literature at Middlebury College's Bread Loaf School of English and her BA in English literature at Smith College. During 2010–11, she was granted a Distinguished Fulbright Award in Teaching.

Lessons I've Learned

If you're someone for whom it's important to have your personal and political values align with those of your workplace, then take the time to find the right workplace.

When I was in high school, we read James Joyce's *Portrait of the Artist as a Young Man* and it spoke to me. He was bullied on the playground; I had been bullied on the playground. He wrote poetry underneath his blankets at night; I also wrote poetry. He was a voracious reader who went off to college and began to question the Catholic church; I had grown up in a

Puerto Rican Catholic household and was also starting to question all kinds of things. I thought, "I wonder why there isn't a book like this about a Puerto Rican girl growing up in New York? I would like to know that girl's story."

I began reading what women wrote about being young artists and discovered feminist theory through Simone de Beauvoir and Kate Millett and Sandra Gilbert and Susan Gubar—but they were all white women. Later, when I first arrived at college, I negotiated my way into a Latina and Latin American Women Writers class (officially closed to first-year students) and finally read books that I'd been waiting for all my life.

Cherríe Moraga's *Loving in the War Years* was the biggest turning point for me, because I had never read a book that provided the language for understanding Latina identity, queer identity, and "brownness." I felt like she was giving me the language that I'd always needed just by naming these parts of herself and saying that all of them could exist together. It made me feel alive. I felt as though I was no longer alone; Moraga and other writers ultimately became important touchstones for understanding struggles that I was going through.

I wanted to bring voices like Moraga out to the world, to let others know that their experiences were reflected through great literature—and so I decided to become an educator. I never wanted my students to feel as though their voices were left out, because I think that there's a kind of invisibility and psychic loneliness students feel when their experiences aren't reflected in the curriculum. One of my first teaching jobs was at a girls' school outside of Washington, DC. From the beginning, I wanted to engage the English department in discussions about the lack of color and queer authors in the curriculum. I also wanted students to read literature that reflected parts of history, such as the Holocaust. The texts that I was suggesting were not that radical, at least to me. I thought our middle school girls should read *Night* by Elie Wiesel, for example, and that our high school program should include Latina and African American writers. There was a bit of pushback from some faculty members, and I couldn't understand why we couldn't engage in a thoughtful conversation about what we were teaching our students.

I'd been there for about two years when the department chair asked to meet with me privately. I thought we were going to talk about my ideas, but our meeting wound up being something entirely different. She brought me into her classroom, which was one of the nicest in the building—it had a carpet, and its windows looked out on the school's well-tended, green athletic fields. A circle of empty desks sat waiting for us, and she gestured for me to sit in one. She sat and handed me a letter that she'd written to me, typed in a small, single-spaced font. It was three pages long.

"Could you read this?" she asked.

I was twenty-five years old and didn't feel like I had the authority or power to ask my department chair whether I could read it by myself and then reconvene to talk, so I sat and read the letter in front of her. It was peppered with phrases like "It seems you're being self-righteous," and "There's a bit of arrogance in your approach." Further along in the letter, she wrote that my interest in introducing new books into the curriculum was "bringing down the morale of the department."

I remember thinking, "This doesn't seem right." I knew that the letter had somehow shifted the power dynamic; it felt wrong to be reading it right in front of her when my understanding had been that we would be having a conversation. I also didn't think that what was being said about how I had introduced new ideas was fair. After I finished reading the letter, I felt my insides shaking. I realized that what she had written was a substitute for true dialogue.

She asked me if I understood what she was trying to say and I said yes, though I only responded that way because I was in shock that this was going to be the extent of our conversation. She then expressed that she was not just sharing her view but that some of the other teachers in the department had approached her saying they thought I was being inappropriate in asking for changes to the curriculum. "Why hadn't those teachers talked to me?" I thought. I apologized and said that any ideas I had shared or e-mails I had written were in the spirit of creating dialogue and were not meant to offend veteran teachers. After our meeting was over, she asked for the letter back, which was yet another way of controlling the entire conversation from beginning to end.

I think back on this moment a lot because there are things

that I could have done differently. I wish I'd had the where-withal during the meeting to say, "I should read this letter on my own and then get back to you; also, I would like a copy." To this day, I still do not have proof of it! But I was too young and scared, still trying to navigate the politics of teaching.

I've also learned that when you're trying to change an in-stitution (like a school), you have to find your allies, people who are like-minded and share your values. Those people are always there but it takes time to find them. Ideally, I should have partnered with a veteran teacher, perhaps even in another department, who could demonstrate that I wasn't just "this er-rant teacher doing something on her own," but instead a teacher who was seeking out others to work with in innovative ways. Maybe then the department chair would have under-stood that others agreed that the curriculum lacked important voices, and maybe I would have avoided that terrible moment of sitting down with her. About a year after that meeting, I did find an ally, someone in the theater department who became a very important partner and advocate. He and I wound up team-teaching classes and even got some women playwrights into the curriculum together.

My five years at that school were the most formative of my teaching career. I cut my teeth there, learning how to write a syllabus and design a course; I also learned important class-room management strategies. But I also closed my classroom door and introduced students to the texts I wanted them to read—which meant that the sit-down with my department chair was just the first of many times that I was told my curriculum didn't align with the mission of the school. Even though I was later approved to teach a course on African American and Latina women writers, by then, I had already become exhausted emotionally and physically.

And there's another layer to this. During that time, I was afraid to come out as queer because I felt as though I was continually on probation, as if I was being watched. As a Latina teacher in an English department, I was already someone the school culture was not used to; parents used to ask me if I was the Spanish teacher. So coming out as a woman of color who was also queer seemed dangerous; I thought it would further push me into more observation from the school and into more isolation in my classroom. It didn't feel safe to tell colleagues I was queer, and I worried that my students—with whom I had great relationships—would reject me. At the same time, it felt so hypocritical: my whole mission in teaching at a girls' school was to empower young women to understand who they were and to become self-actualized, and there I was not modeling that for them.

I began a job search to find a place where I could be me, collaborate with others, bring multiple voices into the curriculum, and also have some autonomy. I found it at Elisabeth Irwin High School, in New York City's Greenwich Village. The high school is part of the Little Red School House, which was founded by a fellow Smith alumna, Elisabeth Irwin, in 1921. Elisabeth Irwin was a progressive educator, a member of John

Dewey's circle of forward-minded teachers, and she was also a lesbian. Even though we were separated by over a half century, I knew that her identity as a progressive lesbian educator was a sign that I should teach at her school.

Once I was working there, I came out, bit by bit. First I was open with a few colleagues, and then it eventually came up in the classroom because for the first time in my life, I was meeting students who were already out. When I taught a queer Latina student who needed someone to mentor her because she was floundering, I thought, "I cannot live a lie in front of this student." Teaching her was an essential part of what inspired me to be a whole person in the classroom.

At Elisabeth Irwin, I've had the chance to collaborate with like-minded colleagues who believe that teaching high school isn't just about instructing students in skills—although that's very important—but that it's also about giving them the tools to transform themselves and the world. It's life-changing to find a school where administrators and colleagues have faith in you and where you can develop a level of comfort that allows you to thrive as a professional and as a woman who can finally be self-actualized not only for herself but also for her students. And I think that's important to find, regardless of your career— because only when you're comfortable with yourself will you thrive.

ILEANA JIMÉNEZ'S TIPS

▶ Realizing that a workplace may not be the right fit
can be a trying and even hurtful experience. The
search for a place that fit my values involved a combination of reflective work with a career counselor and
networking with others who were already in con-
texts that appealed to me. Once I knew what I
was looking for, I was able to target my research
as well as connect with those in my field who could
support my job search, especially other progressive
teachers and those attending job fairs for teachers
of color.

▶ A lot of young people who want to do social justice
work think, "I'm going to embark on this journey
of changing the world by myself!" It took me some
time to realize that the best work is done in collabora-
tion.

▶ Finding allies who are like-minded can sometimes
be daunting. I've found allies and mentors by sharing my work at conferences, especially ones outside
of my field. Cross-pollinating in different spaces
allows for a larger network to emerge, giving rise
to unexpected mentoring and innovative alliances,
including opportunities that align with one's
values.

▶ Being a whole person at work is crucial for feeling
affirmed and being productive. For both people of

color and LGBT people in the workplace, feelings of
isolation are not unusual. Finding professional groups
and events that focus on supporting people of color
and the LGBT community have been essential forms
of self-care.

LISA LUTZ

"It never occurred to me to try to write a perfect book, or one that was better than another writer's book. I just thought, 'I'm going to write a book,' and I knew it would be one that no one else could write, because no one else is me."

Lisa Lutz is loosely categorized as a crime writer, but her mysteries about the Spellman family are also very funny. Her most important influences are comedians like Mel Brooks and Sarah Silverman. "When I was a child I was always drawn to comedy and comedians, and I continue to obsess over whatever impossible formula it is that ends with a laugh," she told Crimespreemag.com.

Lutz is the *New York Times* bestselling author of *The Spellman Files*, *Curse of the Spellmans*, *Revenge of the Spellmans*, *The Spellmans Strike Again*, *Trail of the Spellmans*, *The Last Word*, *Heads You Lose* (with David Hayward), and a children's book, *How to Negotiate Everything* (illustrated by Jaime Temairik). She has won the Alex Award and has been nominated for the Edgar Award for Best Novel.

Lutz never earned a bachelor's degree, even though she attended UC Santa Cruz, UC Irvine, the University of Leeds in England, and San Francisco State University. She spent most of the 1990s writing a screenplay called *Plan B*, which was a mob farce. (Her *Salon* article detailing that process, "Confessions of a Hollywood Sellout," is a must-read.) After *Plan B* was actually made into a film in 2000, Lutz knew she would never write another screenplay.

Lessons I've Learned

Be flexible in thinking about how to use your talents.

I grew up with a stepdad who was a hard-ass, the type of person who was actively cruel to people who made mistakes. Even as a child, I recognized how messed up that was. I saw the ways in which he interacted with others, and I thought, "You're mean—and *that's* a mistake." In fact, I learned social comportment by watching my parents' behavior and deciding to behave in the opposite way. I didn't see any benefit in trying to get everything just so, and I saw *not* being perfect as a way to take a stand against his severity: "I'm just gonna fuck up everything."

So while my stepdad could hurt my feelings, I didn't *feel* criticism from him or from my mother in the way other kids might have from their parents. I knew they were crazy, and so they couldn't flatten me the way other people (like teachers) actually could. It's partly because of my upbringing that I don't relate to that "perfect gene" that some people have—people who have to complete everything on their to-do lists, or alphabetize their books. And I know that the way I am is partly what has allowed me to write; I've noticed that perfectionistic writers who expect too much from themselves can become paralyzed. Meanwhile, great things can come from mistakes and failures, and I can look to my own life as an example: the total train wreck of my first screenplay is what led to my current career as a novelist.

After reading the script for a friend's film during college, I was inspired to try writing my own. I graduated and kept writing screenplays, working day jobs to support myself. One of them, *Plan B*, was about a woman who accidentally gets involved with the mob. Every time she's supposed to kill someone, she drives the victim to her brother's house in Florida. A few years after I got an agent, there was some interest in the script and I optioned it for one dollar to a production company, meaning I gave the company exclusive rights to make it. They had me revise the script at least ten times. When they finally got a deal to actually make the film, I did two more revisions— one paid and one unpaid—but I was fired and a different screenwriter was hired to revise the script *yet again*. Even so, the studio eventually decided to pass. My agent kept shopping the script around, and it was finally bought by a new studio. At this point, I had written at least twenty-five drafts, which had made the script very good (I thought). But this final studio took the script away from me and butchered it; then they set a budget that was too low. The resulting film, made in 2000, was an epic disaster.

It had a brief release in theaters and played in a couple of small festivals, but when the *Hollywood Reporter* called its dialogue "torturously unfunny," I knew that my career as a screenwriter was over. No one was going to want to make a film from something that I wrote. When I considered this, I felt both deep sorrow and a creeping sense of relief. Screenwriting had been my vocation, and letting go of it felt like a real loss; on the other hand, here was an opportunity to think more broadly about what I was going to do with my life.

I began talking to people about my next step, and one was a friend who worked in marketing at Penguin Books. She read what I thought was actually my best screenplay—*The Spellman Files*—and loved it. "Why don't you write this as a novel?" she asked.

It hadn't occurred to me, but I decided to give it a shot, because I had run out of options. Essentially, I wrote a novel as a last resort. I started the book while working as a secretary at my uncle's CPA practice. (During tax season, I literally stapled for a living.) But working full-time made writing a novel feel like an insurmountable task, so I ended up saving some money and my relatives let me borrow their empty house in upstate New York. I drove there in September and returned in April with a novel. Because there were so many rules in screenwriting, I decided that when I wrote the novel there would be no rules. I figured if I could get the reader to turn the page, I was doing my job. I just wanted to write the most engaging book I could. This freed me to think beyond traditional novel structure. There's nothing about *The Spellman Files* that is traditional. It doesn't fit properly into a genre: it includes lists, transcripts, dossiers, and footnotes. I remember when I was writing the book, I felt a bit unhinged, but also alive.

To my pleasure, *The Spellman Files* was a success, becoming a *New York Times* bestseller. My publisher arranged for a huge book tour, and I was invited to speak all over the world. I was so used to failure with the screenplays that it never, ever occurred to me I'd wake up one day with six novels under my belt. Some days, I still feel like, "How did this happen?"

Prepare for public speaking events. If you don't know how to work a crowd, then get help!

I knew that I was supposed to be excited about my very first book tour, but I dreaded it. I didn't tell anyone because I knew I was lucky to get this book deal and wanted to do whatever my publisher asked, but I remember just staring into my empty suitcase, thinking that I had no idea how to dress for a speech I had to give with several other writers in front of the Junior League in Virginia.

Not only did I have no idea what to wear, I had no idea what to talk about. When I had asked my publicist what the speech should be about, she'd basically said, "Whatever." She seemed to think it was obvious, but to me, it wasn't. Why did people want to hear me talk in the first place? And what did they want to know? I went with what was foremost in my mind and wrote a speech about not having a speech, even adding the little story about asking for help and not getting any. I tucked the speech into my suitcase, still feeling that it wasn't quite it, and boarded the flight to Virginia.

That night, there was a dinner for the panelists, a group of seasoned writers. It turned out that I was the only author touring for her first book, and as I sat at the dinner table listening to them discuss the speeches *they* were going to give, I stopped chewing my food. I was unable to move, even to lift my fork. "Oh, no," I thought. "Oh, no." My heart was beating rapidly and I realized that I was having a complete panic attack.

Someone looked over at me and asked, "Lisa, are you okay?"

I whispered, "I was just going to talk about not having a speech." Immediately, everyone at the table got quiet. Clearly, this wasn't going to fly.

"This is what people want to know," said Steve Roberts, a reporter (and Cokie Roberts's husband), who was going to be emceeing the event the next day. "What's your writing process like? How did you get here?" He asked those questions as if they were no big deal, as if the answers were on the tip of my tongue *already*. They weren't. Steve told me to go to my room that night and work on the speech and he'd coach me the next day.

I sat at the tiny hotel room desk, scrawling on a yellow legal pad as the digital clock clicked to eleven, then twelve, then one. Finally I had what I thought was a draft of an actual speech.

In the morning, Steve kindly sat with me over coffee in the dining room, looking over what I'd written, offering suggestions—cut this, you need a little more of that. He told me what was funny—I had a short anecdote about the ancient house I lived in, which was where I'd written the book, and he suggested I add more. I went back to my hotel room and rewrote it *again*.

And suddenly it was time. The panelists gathered backstage, and then we were ushered on. When I saw the size of the audience, I spun around and started walking back out: there were sixteen hundred people sitting there. An audience of fifty was the largest I'd spoken to on my tour, and that was because my family and everyone I knew had come to see me at a bookstore in L.A. Even then I'd been nervous, but this was horrendous. I remember two of the writers just grabbing me and turning me back, saying, "You've got to do this."

But here's the amazing thing. I gave the speech and it went well. While I was talking, I wasn't really nervous; in fact, I found that I actually *liked* telling these people about how I'd become a writer. They were clearly tuned in, enthusiastic about me and about my book. Plus, my road to authorship was a true underdog story and people tend to respond to that sort of thing.

Since then, public speaking has been a mixed bag for me. When I'm on panels with other authors, they're sometimes very generous and sometimes not; sometimes the moderator is great and sometimes not. There can be a sense of competition on panels, which I don't like, and I often feel as if I'm the least eloquent one so I end up just getting really quiet. But I've figured out that my favorite way to speak with an audience is to be as informal as possible. When I put myself in their shoes, I think: "Would I want to be trapped in a room, listening to me talk?" Even the best public speakers can become boring. If I engage the audience, even going right to Q&A, it kind of shakes things up. There's a sense of not knowing what's going to happen, and for some reason that makes me feel *less* nervous.

I think that audiences "get" that I'm comfortable enough with myself to allow for some openness in my conversations with them, and they generally respond well. I'm glad that I was also comfortable enough to let go of screenplays and try my hand in a format about which I really knew nothing. It's what led to my success as a writer. In general, a lot of good can come from *not* needing to be in control of everything. I would encourage every young woman to find at least one beautifully mucky place in which you're *not* the expert—and then to wade in.

LISA LUTZ'S TIPS

▶ When it comes to public speaking, the most important thing to remember is that people don't come to watch you fail. Care more about the subject than your ego.

▶ People are comfortable with others who are open about their flaws, who don't try to pretend to be more than they are. It's easier to go through life being honest and owning up to your less-than qualities than faking it.

KIM GORDON

"As a woman, you're in a constant state of 'catching up.' I felt like this because I had a career and a child, but also because even though I was playing music, I have always thought of myself as a visual artist."

K im Gordon invited me to conduct our interview in her roomy old house on a quiet street in Northampton, Massachusetts. I came in through the back door and porch, where Gordon shushed two barking mutts. Sitting at a table in front of a light-filled bay window, she began the conversation on "mistakes" by saying she'd just been thinking about the pressure that women can feel "to do everything." Gordon would know—she has certainly done a lot.

Kim Gordon became known for being part of the band Sonic Youth with her former husband, Thurston Moore. An early review in the *New York Times* described the band by saying, "Sonic Youth tears rock apart from the inside out," that it "simply ignores everyone else's rules." Seemingly without thinking much of it, Gordon gradually became a role model for a whole generation of girls and young women—and boys and young men, for that matter—who wanted to create music outside of the confines of traditional rock 'n' roll. She didn't start playing bass until she was in her late twenties; now she's held up as one of the female icons of 1990s-era rock music, and although in recent years her marriage ended and Sonic Youth disbanded, Gordon has continued to make both music and art. With collaborator Bill Nace she formed Body/Head and released an album called *Coming Apart* in 2013; she's also working on a memoir.

Lessons I've Learned

Even when you're certain of your path from a young age, it's good to be open to opportunity and possibility—and to the idea that having a career doesn't have to mean doing one thing for your whole life.

A lot of people in high school or college don't know what they want to do; I always did. In fact, an old friend of my parents says that I'm exactly the same person as I was when I was five years old, making little clay elephants. I always wanted to be an artist, even though I didn't really know what that meant.

In the early 1980s, I came to New York to do art. I got a job at a gallery and witnessed what was really an art explosion.

Suddenly a lot of people were buying pieces from these young artists, who were like rock stars. I soon realized that I didn't like being in that world, where art was becoming a high-end consumer object being sold to wealthy people. There's nothing wrong with that in itself, but when you're making art, it can feel disheartening.

A friend, Dan Graham, introduced me to music. Dan was a music critic and an artist, and through him I learned about the No Wave movement, which was dissonant, expressionistic music. It was influenced by minimalism and was more nihilistic than punk rock. Dan encouraged me to write, and I wrote this very short essay, "Trash Drugs and Male Bonding," for a magazine called *Real Life*. The essay was about the phenomenon of male musicians being into a drug called "locker room," which was really just amyl nitrate. They'd take a hit and then double down on the guitar in this minimalist way, and I wanted to describe that I noticed it afforded them a certain kind of camaraderie. In general, playing music has often allowed men to show their female side; I think of Mick Jagger prancing around the stage like Tina Turner, for example, in such an emotional and expressive way.

I would go with Dan to see shows, but soon I started to think that I'd like to be more in the middle of it instead of being a voyeur. It seemed very free and I thought, "I can do that." I started playing music with friends and around 1981, Dan invited me to play in a performance piece that he was doing: with a mirror onstage, Dan would describe the audience looking at him and describe himself looking at the audience. Because he was writing music criticism about all-girl groups, he wanted one to actually be in the piece and asked me if I'd join some female friends of his to do that. I said yes. He introduced me to Christine and Miranda, and after we were in his show at the ICA in Boston, we kept getting together to play music. Miranda introduced me to Thurston Moore and we soon formed Sonic Youth.

Initially, I was inspired by all the women in the punk and No Wave scenes in the late seventies. In the eighties, there weren't a lot of women in music, but I was a tomboy and used to being around guys, so I didn't really think about it much. When we started touring in England, people would ask what it was like for me to be the only woman in Sonic Youth, and I thought, "Well, it's not like I'm in a band with a bunch of smelly jocks or frat guys."

My role in Sonic Youth was unique partly because I wasn't a performer in the way that other punk musicians were. In England especially, they each had a punk persona expressed by one style or outfit—almost dressing as characters. Siouxsie Sioux, for example, was "witchy." Even Patti Smith was somewhat stylized in this sort of spiritual way. I thought they were amazing, but I had come from a middle-class background, and for me being in Sonic Youth was really about the music and about having a presence onstage. I came to understand that I didn't have to be some freakazoid to be a performer or a singer; I could just be a girl and that was enough. So my

"persona" was just me, and while I'm interested in the relationship between the performer and the audience, I've always
been conscious about not wanting to exploit that. It was enough
to be there in the middle of things, with the electricity swarm-
ing around me.

Looking back, I think that I went into music partly to escape the art world—so that I wouldn't have to buy into the
idea of what a "successful artist" must be. Music, and especially the music that I got involved with, actually seemed like
a freer form of expression. I didn't really have any knowledge
about it; I'd internalized *something* from my record collection
but my understanding of music just wasn't "studied," so I was
able to work less conceptually than I did as an artist, and less
self-consciously.

I have been able to have a certain art practice, and now
that Sonic Youth is over, I can devote myself to it more fully. A
lot of painters have a certain *thing* they do that's recognizable,
and then they develop it and morph it. I'm not really interested
in that. I could understand making a series of pieces that are
similar, but I couldn't see confining myself to my one recognizable "thing." I'm interested in art that looks like a mistake—
for example, paintings that are sort of baggy, or pieces that
don't even look like art—because then it's more about the process and meaning of the work and less about "making an art
object," which almost seems to me like doing arts and crafts,
at this point. It's really hard to make a painting that just
kind of breaks through and has some fresh energy—that has

something conceptual going on, separate from the visual nice-
ness of it. Sonic Youth had some cultural significance, and it's
hard to make art with the same kind of significance—but in a
way, that's my goal.

Still, it's not easy to make people set aside that part of my
career in a way that allows me to be taken seriously, so that
my art isn't just an accessory to my life in Sonic Youth. People
are always trying to put me in shows with other musicians
who do art or something—why? I don't even like playing in
festivals with other bands unless I really like them. So I'm still
trying to navigate that, to figure out a way to use it as a subject
matter. I'm not a conventional person, and ultimately I didn't
want a conventional art career. Being in a big gallery is not the
most important thing to me now. It has to be the right gallery.
It has to be the right context. I want to treat my art the way we
treated our music career.

Trying to maintain two careers, visual art and music, and
to be a mother at the same time, always felt kind of impossible.
When you're feeling that you can and should do *everything*,
then you never feel like you're going to achieve *anything*. I
think what kept me going was this deep understanding that it
wasn't going to be perfect, and that it didn't have to be.

KIM GORDON'S TIPS

▶ Know that even if you start out with a certain idea of what you're going to do in your life, almost no one ends up following that straight line.

▶ The idea of "work-life balance" is not necessarily helpful. If you are immersed in your work and raising a family, you might feel a lot of good things—but it may not include "balanced."

▶ You don't have to think, "I do this for work and will *always* do it." Careers are long, and they evolve and change over time. That's actually a good thing.

RESHMA SAUJANI

"After you have a major failure, there is a recovery time. I don't want to be unrealistic and say I woke up the day after my congressional loss and was, like, 'Great, on to the next thing.' Failures are hard on the soul, and I think you have to take steps to emotionally and physically recover. One thing that's important for us—women *and* men—is to really know yourself and your commitments. My calling is public service, but I wasn't elected right away, and that's okay. I don't think anything has ever come easy for me. When that's the case, you appreciate the victory so much more."

Fighting for social justice was a theme in Reshma Saujani's life from a young age. Her family lived in Uganda when she was a young child; as she tells the story, one day Idi Amin came on the radio and told all the Indians that they had ninety days to leave. The United States was the only country that would accept her family as political refugees, and they came to their new home with nothing.

They moved to the Midwest, becoming one of the few Indian families in a town where discrimination was part of the undercurrent of everyday experience. She started doing antibias work at thirteen and continued through college, where she was a part of a group that advocated for an Asian American cultural studies center, and Yale Law School; upon graduation, she worked for Bill Clinton's 1996 campaign.

In 2002, Saujani moved to New York and worked as an attorney by day but also took part in a campaign to mobilize voter registration for South Asians. She decided to pursue public office, and although she didn't win her first campaigns—a run for Congress and a subsequent bid for the role of pubilc advocate—she made sure to create a context in which real social change could happen. Girls Who Code is the nonprofit that she started, on her own, because she didn't want low-income girls to be left behind as New York City drew more and more tech companies—along with the jobs they created. She talks often with these girls about the value of taking risks.

Lessons I've Learned

Take control of the story that you want to tell about yourself.

I ran for Congress in 2009 and was fortunate to have a great group of young people working on my campaign. On the night of the election, I sat in my hotel room with this group, including

a young woman named Rebecca, who was in her early twenties
and had been a traveling campaign manager since the beginning. We were optimistic at first as we watched the results come
in on TV; in fact, I felt so confident that I hadn't even written a
concession speech. As the night wore on, hope faded. It was
clear from the numbers coming back from the polling booth
that it wasn't going well, and I remember one of my staffers saying, "We're going to have to write a speech." I told him that I
thought we still had a chance, but inside I wanted to cry. The
only thing that kept me from doing so was looking over at Rebecca, and thinking that she just might remember this moment
for the rest of her life. I wanted to be a model of strength and
resilience, so I asked her to bring me some paper and a pen and
wrote my speech. At the concession party, I kept it together. I'd
received only 19 percent of the vote, but I told the crowd that I
was proud to have their support and that I wasn't going to give
up. "We ran against the establishment, did what nobody thought
we should do," I told them. "Regardless of the outcome, all of us
are victorious."

The minute I got home, though, I allowed myself to feel
devastated. I had put my personal savings into the race, and
now I was broke. I had made commitments to voters about
what I was going to do in the community, and now I felt like I
had let them down. It was such a public failure, and meanwhile, I hadn't made a plan B. So I told myself that I had two
weeks to feel upset about it, to ask myself why, to harass everybody in my life to analyze what had happened. It was helpful to

set a timeline for obsessing, to allow myself the indulgence and then commit to moving forward.

After about six weeks or so, I began to speak on panels and to audiences about my failure. I just don't think that we model that vulnerability for young people as much as we need to. It's important for people to see that you can pick yourself up and move on. Oftentimes, especially for women, they'll lose a race and then they're just never going to run again, but I had made a commitment to myself that I was not going to do that. I was going to take the steps that were necessary for me to emotionally get into this space that I would run again.

As I reflected on what had gone wrong, I realized that my narrative and *who I was* had gotten lost during my campaign. Because I had spent time working as a lawyer for the financial services industry, I had become known as "the Wall Street candidate." Meanwhile, the reality is that I'm the daughter of political refugees who came to the United States with nothing, and I graduated from law school with two hundred thousand dollars in student loans. Even though I'd always known I wanted to go into service, a series of early jobs on Wall Street helped to pay off that debt (and my parents' mortgage). This story would have resonated with a lot of people, but it got lost. Part of that was due to the social and political climate: the financial crisis had just happened, and here I was, a candidate who had worked on Wall Street—*of course* the conversation would come to be about that. If I could do it over again, I'd be more cognizant of how my background could be misconstrued.

My real life narrative was missing, in part, because I was in such a rush to do my first interview that I didn't stop to reflect on what was important for people to know about me—which would have allowed me to take control of my story. I didn't explain that my time in the financial services industry wasn't because I aspired to be the CEO of a bank; it was because I aspired to be in public service but couldn't afford to follow the traditional lockstep model of going into politics. A job as a junior staffer for a politician wouldn't have allowed me to pay off my student loan debt; you have to come from financial stability to do that. I hadn't felt comfortable telling people that I wasn't from that place, which was a misstep on my behalf.

When I share my story now, young people often come up and tell me that they're in the same situation: They want to do social justice work or serve in government, but they're broke or in debt or they feel an obligation to help their families get to solid economic ground. They ask whether going into the private sector for a while will prevent them from doing what they want later in life, and I tell them that being able to accurately talk about *why* you took the twists and turns is really important.

Find a way to work toward your goal, even if it's not the way you thought you'd do it.

Even within the first week after I lost, I knew that I wanted to continue in public service; I just didn't know what form it would take. I started thinking about opportunities that were open for me to continue the work that I had started, and within a few months I was hired to be the deputy public advocate of New York City. The public advocate promotes government accountability and engages the public in making its needs known.

Within my new role, I soon saw a problem: New York City children in public school did not have proper access to and training in technology. For girls, especially, the statistics were grim, with low percentages pursuing tech education in college and beyond. I decided to start a not-for-profit called Girls Who Code, which teaches computer science to teenage girls from New York City's five boroughs. Girls Who Code wants to ensure that the next generation of women has the necessary skills to go into high-paying industries to move themselves and their families forward.

As I was working to get Girls Who Code up and running, I was also falling in love with the role of public advocate, a position that has the capacity to make real change in people's lives. I decided to run for that office two years after my congressional loss, but this time, to put it all out there. It wasn't easy to tell everyone that I had a lot of student loan debt, and that I had my family to take care of, but the hope was that it would resonate in a meaningful way for people. Even my clothes were different the second time around: in 2010, I wore boxy suits and kept my hair in a ponytail because advisers said that it was important not to draw attention to how you look. It was confining, because if I then dressed more like myself during an interview, that seemed to distract the reporter. A *New York Times* article once mentioned my shoes, for example, and although my immediate thought was, "Oh, my God, I can't believe I broke the rules, I should have dressed more conservatively," I think the *real* takeaway was that I should have just been me the whole time. I was more myself during the 2013 race, and while we didn't win, authenticity mattered: our showing was significantly stronger, and we learned new lessons that we'll take into the next endeavor.

When you have major setbacks, you ironically begin to feel like you can do anything because the worst has already happened and you're no longer paralyzed by the fear of something not working out. If I hadn't run for office, I would never be where I am now, the founder of a successful nonprofit. That's why I tell young people to fail fast, fail hard, and fail often.

RESHMA SAUJANI'S TIPS

▶ We should be able to take new directions in work. One way of smoothing the path for a career change is to take control of your own narrative. I often talk about how I've had several careers already, but my mission has always been the same.

▶ A loss in a run for public office—or in any situation where you're competing for a job—isn't necessarily indicative of how you'd *do* that job, and it doesn't mean you shouldn't keep trying for it. It's the same as when you're starting a company and asking for investment: If your first company doesn't work out, does that mean that you can't still be an entrepreneur or have a successful business? No!

CHERYL STRAYED

"Being a writer means failing every day. It means following the wrong path in order to find the right one. Do you know how many pages I've written that will never be published anywhere?"

In March 2012, I was reading the *New York Times* and came across a glowing review of a new memoir called *Wild* by the author Cheryl Strayed. The reviewer, Dwight Garner, said that the book had made him weep as he sat reading in a café but that it was not cloying. "This book," he wrote, "is as loose and sexy and dark as an early Lucinda Williams song. It's got a punk spirit and makes an earthy and American sound." I had to go out and buy it immediately, and then I couldn't put it down. Apparently, a lot of other people couldn't put down their copies, either; in its debut week in March 2012, *Wild* was already number seven on the national bestseller list. By June, it had become an Oprah pick and shot to number one.

Wild, which tells the story of Cheryl Strayed's hike alone along the Pacific Crest Trail, was the author's second book; her first was a well-received novel, *Torch*. Strayed is also the author of *Tiny Beautiful Things*, a collection of the popular Dear Sugar advice column that she wrote for the *Rumpus*.

Although Strayed had the kind of over-the-top success that

many authors only dream about, she seems both incredibly generous and grounded. Her Facebook page is filled with supportive plugs for writer friends and colleagues with new books or upcoming readings. Because I was so in love with her book, I thought, "It never hurts to ask," and invited her to contribute to mine. She wrote back almost immediately, saying yes.

Lessons I've Learned

Listen to your gut.

The best traditional job I ever had, by which I mean I worked for somebody and they paid me, was when I was a youth advocate for at-risk girls in a middle school. I'd been a waitress for years in order to pay the bills, writing on the side, and I'd gotten to a point where I was becoming angry and bitter about having to serve people food when my true ambitions were as a writer. I decided I needed a job that was actually rewarding, and in working with these girls I got that. I was not only doing work that was enjoyable to me, but I was also changing people's lives. I mean, I could see it: I was actually contributing to society in general and these young women in particular by helping them get on a better path. Nurturing them was something I deeply believed in. Yet, all the while I had a terrible feeling in my gut. I'd think, "Yeah, yeah, this is great, but I *really* should be writing. What I truly have to give the world is my writing." It was instructive to know that even though working with those girls was pretty much as good as it gets professionally—in terms of satisfaction—I still wasn't doing the right thing for me, personally.

It was that job that led me to finally say, "Okay, I'm going to have to do whatever it takes to be a writer full-time." I applied to an MFA program, quit my job, and moved across the country to write and attend Syracuse University. In graduate school, I wrote my first book, *Torch*. Even after I'd sold it, I still needed to take jobs for money, but at that point, they were jobs related to writing, a mix of teaching and freelancing for magazines. Recognizing what was most important to me had helped to set me on a path that felt right.

When you don't connect with the work that you're doing, it can feel nearly impossible to get it done.

The lesson I've learned over and over again as a writer is that my work has to come from an authentic place. It's impossible for me to fake it on the page. This isn't to say I've never had to push myself to write about something that doesn't come particularly easily to me—doing so is certainly part of being a writer. But I've learned that I can't pretend I have something to say when I don't. This was made deeply apparent to me several years ago when I accepted an assignment from *Allure* magazine to write about my "signature scent." Signature scent? I didn't even know what that was, so I certainly didn't have one. Perfume makes me queasy. But I was broke and the job paid well so I said yes.

Immediately I went off to find myself a signature scent. I went to a store that specializes in just this thing—in matching people with the perfect cologne or perfume. I walked in and told the woman behind the counter that I needed to find a fragrance I could love. As I sampled this and that, I pretended I didn't feel like I was about to puke. After thirty minutes I made my choice, paid for the perfume with my almost-at-the-limit credit card, and went home to my husband and newborn son. As soon as I walked through the door, my husband made a terrible face and asked what I was wearing. "My new signature scent," I replied and smiled.

I wore the perfume every day for the next several days, trying to fall in love with it so I could write honestly about how much it meant to me, but it was a lie. I did not have a signature scent and I never would. I couldn't bring myself to pretend, no matter how many dollars I received for each word. I flailed and I floundered and then finally I decided to do what I do best in my writing: tell the truth. I wrote about my relationship to fragrances over the years, my childhood longing for them that gave way to my adult disdain. My essay culminated in the fact that I don't have a signature scent, but I happily carry the odors of my ordinary life—the smells of children's hair or the hand soap I use, the lavender that grows in my yard.

I was able to salvage the piece while holding on to my integrity. It was a big lesson for me. When you're taking a job because you need the money, at least when it comes to writing, you still have to be able to sincerely apply yourself to the assignment. We all need to pay the bills—that's part of life. But we also need to acknowledge that when a task feels so wrong it's paralyzing, that's important information to be aware of. Sometimes it means we simply need to be creative within the confines of the assignment, as I was when writing that essay about my nonexistent signature scent. Other times, it means that we need to find different work.

Feedback is scary, but it makes your work better.

The writing that's been most lucrative for me, the most successful by any measure, is the writing that I would've done even if it had never been published or purchased by anyone. I was paid nothing for the Dear Sugar column—which became the book *Tiny Beautiful Things*—but I loved writing it. My novel, *Torch*, and memoir, *Wild*, were both written with no guarantee that I'd be paid for them. I'd have written them even if no one had opted to publish them. They've brought me success I wouldn't have imagined; I bought a house recently and every penny of it was paid for by *Wild*. My husband and I were stunned. We kept saying to each other, "What? How did *that* happen?" In the arts, you need to learn not to expect that success will equal money. There were whole years when I was writing my first two books during which my husband and I qualified for food stamps, even though we didn't apply for them. We were constantly under financial pressure—he's an artist, too, a filmmaker. Unless you have someone else supporting you, you have to be prepared to take risks, financial and otherwise.

Making a commitment to writing or art requires taking the long view. You have to say, "Okay, it's not paying this week or this month, or even this year, but if I stick with it maybe someday it will." You have to ask yourself what a career in the arts looks like over ten years or twenty years. And even then you don't know. The only path to success is keeping the faith.

A key piece of keeping the faith has to do with dealing with rejection. It's a part of any profession in the arts, all along the way. It's not like you get rejected at the beginning of your career and then you achieve this state where everything you do is greeted with applause. There will always be something you didn't get that you wanted, some recognition or prize or award. Even when things aren't rejected, you have to endure a sense that all may have failed. You're always starting anew, with every book or essay or story. Doubt is a part of the writer's life. Every time my Dear Sugar column would go up on the Web, I'd wonder, "Is this one going to be the one that makes everyone say, 'You suck. You're terrible'?" With both *Torch* and *Wild*, when I sent them off to my editor, I was sick with fear and anxiety and uncertainty. In both cases, the editor came back and said, "Overall, it's great—but here are all the things that aren't great about it, things you should reconsider or that aren't working." That's what editors do—it's their job to help us make our work better.

The revision process is humbling because you must listen to people who are telling you honestly what they think of this work you've poured your whole heart into and sometimes spent years producing. It's very stressful and sometimes hurtful, too, but receiving criticism is part of the writer's job. You have to learn how not to be defeated by a long editorial letter outlining all the things an editor finds fault with—"I don't think this scene is working" or "You've gone too far here." And there's an extra layer of vulnerability when the book is a memoir because there's no hiding. It's about *you*. Cheryl Strayed in *Wild* is a literary construct, sure, but she's still *me*. I've had to learn not to take critiques of my work personally— as it's certainly not meant to be. I've learned to trust that the people who are on my side are being honest for the very reason that they *are* on my side—not because they want to destroy me. There's no question that my editor's feedback made *Wild* a better book.

I think the revision process is a great metaphor for how to approach life and love and work. We're all rough drafts. If you're living right you're constantly striving to make the next version of yourself one notch better. Real success is rooted in learning how to turn mistakes into successes; losses into gains; failures into the things of value that propel you forward rather than hold you back. My advice is to be humble, to listen to

those who have more experience than you do, to work hard—
actually hard—and also to trust yourself. No one makes your
life for you. You make it for yourself.

CHERYL STRAYED'S TIPS

▶ If you're any kind of artist, you're going to have rejection all along the way, but if at least *some* of what
you're working on sustains you, it will help you to be
resilient and to keep going.

▶ Sometimes you have to do jobs to pay the bills. I did
that for years—I mean, I certainly didn't feel "called"
to be a waitress. But there was no way I could have
become a writer if I hadn't had a lot of jobs that allowed me to put my real energy into my writing.

▶ Sometimes people feel like they *should* be writers because it's cool or because their friends are writers. I've
had students like this and I think, "You don't really
want to be a writer, and it's okay to do something
else." Spend time figuring out what is ideal for you,
not what others expect of you. Whatever it is that's
your thing, pursue that with relentless passion.

PART II

Learning to Ask

As I was putting together this book, my secret code name for it was "the Chutzpah Project," *chutzpah* being the Yiddish word for guts or courage. I thought about it as I e-mailed each contributor and asked if she'd talk about her most important mistakes; I thought about it as I probed people to tell me about some personal experience or difficult situation or feeling. Was I asking too much? One contributor said that she felt vulnerable telling her story; she wasn't sure if she even wanted me to include it. But it was a story that I loved, one that I thought would be useful to readers, so I urged her to let me keep it in and she generously consented. She's brave, I thought. "You've got *some* chutzpah," I told myself.

* * *

Apparently, "asking" can be tricky for women. We most often hear about this within the context of salary. In a lecture that she gave at Smith, journalist and radio host Farai Chideya talked about a friend she had whose job was to negotiate contracts. "Anytime that he offered people promotions," she said, "every white man asked for more money and no women and no people of color asked for more money." Stories like this are borne out in research. Linda Babcock and Sara Laschever's bestseller, *Women Don't Ask*, revealed that women are perfectly good negotiators on the behalf of others, but that we're less likely than men to ask *for ourselves*. Babcock and another colleague, Hannah Riley Bowles, have since demonstrated that women may be penalized for asking in ways that supervisors—both male and female—see as too aggressive. In a 2011 NPR interview, Babcock called this "depressing" but recommended that women who want to use her research to help them get what they want should try a negotiating manner that's "friendly, warm, and concerned for others above yourself."

If hearing this makes you want to throw in the towel on negotiating (or maybe to throw up?), consider this: the American Association of University Women looked at the average starting salary of a *male* recent graduate, compared it to a female peer's, and calculated that his female peer is likely making about $2,800 less than he is. This could buy "nearly a year's worth of groceries, over 750 gallons of gas or 1,400 tall Starbucks coffees." It could also cover twelve months of student loan payments. So despite the fact that it often feels hard to ask, despite the fact that it's complicated by icky data showing that it behooves female negotiators to smile (etc.)—it's *really* worth negotiating that first salary.

And practicing negotiation is not only good for our bank accounts; it can serve our educational and career ambitions, as Selena Rezvani discusses in her interview. It can benefit our relationships with friends, roommates, and romantic partners. Once you have kids, it's great to be able to identify your *own* needs—for time to work, exercise, meditate, be with friends, be alone, sleep, etc. Asking for, and then ideally *getting*, what you need is often healthy for the entire family.

Sometimes, when we're starting off in our professional lives, we can't imagine asking for *anything*. A professor I know told me that she once came out of her office to find a student just standing there, waiting for what had probably been more than a few minutes. "I wasn't sure if you were in there," the student said. But even when we're standing with our hands poised at the proverbial door, we can learn to knock firmly and loudly, to become good advocates for ourselves over the course of our careers. In the following

interviews, contributors discuss learning to ask for
opportunities, advice, or information—and to not be
afraid of appearing ignorant. They are good models for all
of us, and their message is strong: a little chutzpah is not a
bad thing.

DANIELLE OFRI

"It's easy to feel like you're either a good or bad doctor—and that those are the only two choices. When I meet with students, I talk about errors, owning up to those I've made and letting them know that it's a part of life. I hope that later on, when one of them makes an error, he or she thinks, 'My attending talked about this—it's a normal part of learning to be a doctor and I don't have to hide it.'"

When I spoke with Danielle Ofri, she had just come from a celebration at her son's school in New York City. It was midmorning and she was on her way to her job as a clinician at Bellevue Hospital, one of the city's busiest hospitals, with a diverse and often poor patient population. When she's not at Bellevue, Ofri teaches medical students; she is an associate professor at New York University School of Medicine. Needless to say, she's a very busy woman. But despite the intensity of her work, her interaction with patients and students seems to be a natural source of stories for her, and she's penned several books on her life in medicine. Her newest book is called *What Doctors Feel: How Emotions Affect the Practice of Medicine.* Others include *Medicine in Translation: Journeys with My Patients, Incidental Findings: Lessons from My Patients in the*

Art of Medicine, and *Singular Intimacies: Becoming a Doctor at Bellevue.*

Ofri holds both an MD and a PhD and writes regularly for the *New York Times* about being a doctor and about the relationship between doctors and patients. Her essays have twice appeared in *Best American Essays* and have been published in *Best American Science Writing.* She is the recipient of the John P. McGovern Award from the American Medical Writers Association for "preeminent contributions to medical communication."

Lessons I've Learned

You and your bad decision are two separate things.

A medical residency is three years. The first year is hard, but as an intern, you follow orders and are not technically responsible for anything. Second-year residents, though, take on much more responsibility, acting as team leaders for the interns and medical students. This story is about my first time being in charge, the first time I actually had to make a medical decision that would affect a patient's well-being.

Soon after the start date of my second year of residency, a patient came in with diabetic ketoacidosis—otherwise known as DKA. The patient had type 1 diabetes, and he'd been arrested. While he was held he was unable to access his insulin;

his sugar levels skyrocketed and knocked him unconscious. Treating DKA is fascinating and immensely gratifying: the patient comes in comatose or nearly so, and the doctor administers an IV insulin drip to slowly lower the sugar, carefully monitoring electrolytes as well as acid and potassium levels in the blood. If it's done correctly, the patient is miraculously cured within twenty-four hours.

When we had done all this with my patient and he was awake and alert, we prepared to turn off the IV. As I handed the "d/c insulin drip" order to the nurse, she asked, "Do you want to give an injection of long-acting insulin before I turn off the drip?"

I thought about it.

I turned to my intern, who was standing beside me, and said, "We've just spent an entire day meticulously controlling this patient's sugar. Why would we want a big dose of long-acting insulin? It will be like a sledgehammer, staying in his system for hours and bottoming out his sugar. Let's just stop the drip and check his sugar regularly. We'll keep injecting him with small amounts as needed."

The nurse raised an eyebrow, but I didn't pay much attention. I was *the doctor*, after all.

Within two hours, the patient began to feel nauseous and to vomit. I realized that his potassium level was falling, his acid level was rising, and we were in trouble. As I called the medical consult, the senior resident in charge for the night, the patient started slurring his speech and getting woozy. When the medical consult arrived, she looked at the patient's numbers, thought for about three seconds, and yelled:

"Didn't you give him long-acting insulin before you turned off the drip? This guy could go into cardiac arrest—what were you *thinking?*"

I froze. What *had* I been thinking? Had I forgotten the part about long-acting insulin? Had I never learned it? My intern didn't say a word. The medical consult gave me a withering, granitic stare as I tried to explain my logic—but suddenly I could not put two words together. Just an hour before, I had confidently told the intern, "Long-acting insulin will do bad things to this patient," and he had followed me so trustingly.

The three of us stood in the middle of the ER trauma section, chaos all around us: gunshot victims were being wheeled in; surgeons and nurses were running everywhere. The senior resident stared at me, holding me in this spot, and still I couldn't talk. I could have evaporated, or fallen dead of a cardiac arrest, and I would have been grateful. It was the most humiliating experience I'd ever had—because I saw my error clearly: the very thing you're *supposed* to do before turning off the drip is to give a shot of long-acting insulin so that it stays in the patient's system. If you don't, then the patient goes right back into DKA, which was exactly what my patient had done.

The senior resident finally grabbed the sheet out of my hand and barked, "Restart the drip and give him stat doses of calcium and bicarb to prevent cardiac arrest," quickly doing these things herself to save the patient's life. Then she stormed off, and I was left standing there with my intern right next to me.

I stammered, "Well, let's just, uh . . . get some labs on this patient." The intern was absolutely matter-of-fact. He took out the blood test tubes and started writing the labels; looking back, I see that the normalcy of his actions was so compassionate. I was never able to thank him, but the fact that he just kept going allowed me to keep going. If he had tried to talk about it, if he had acted embarrassed or walked away, I don't think I could have continued as his leader in the same way. But he could see how humiliated I was, and he gave me the respect of listening to what little authority I had left, as if he were saying, "I still trust your leadership."

Luckily, the patient was fine, even though he had to spend another day in the ICU. I, on the other hand, didn't fare so well. It took weeks to pick myself up off the floor, and there was no one to talk to about it. If my attending physician at the time had let me know that errors do happen, and had said something like "An error doesn't mean you're a bad person—it means you're a human being," that would have meant a lot. But I didn't hear that sort of sentiment, and so instead, the incident played over and over again on loop in my head.

I've since thought a lot about the difference between guilt and shame. Guilt relates to an act you did, and you can remedy that act to resolve the guilt. But shame is internal; it's the realization that you're not who you thought you were. Guilt makes you want to fix things, but shame makes you want to run and hide. And shame was what I had felt as I stood there in the ER being reprimanded.

Senior doctors need to come forward and talk about

errors, about how they dealt with the shame and how they maintained their sense of self. They need to talk about how they approached their patients and acknowledged their medical errors. It's not easy; it was only recently that I first wrote about the episode described above—and that was twenty years after it happened. But I learned two important things from that mistake. One: Thou shalt not turn off the insulin drip before injecting long-acting insulin. I teach that to every student I have, and if any of my patients are on insulin drips, I'm like a hawk, checking on them all the time. Two: Errors should be corrected, but humiliating someone doesn't do anything. Because yes, the patient's safety comes first and doctors must do what they can in order to act in their best interest, but you don't learn a lesson any better through humiliation. In fact, it may be damaging.

If I want to tell a colleague or student about an error, I pull that person aside and do it in private whenever possible. If we're in the middle of an emergency and I need to correct something in public for the sake of my patient, I will of course act within that moment, but then afterward I'll take that person aside and say, "You're a fine doctor—smart, committed, caring. But here's one place where a mistake was made." It's important to help that person make a distinction—it's not that *you* were wrong, it's that your decision was wrong. Whatever job you're in, whether you make a mistake as a doctor or a teacher or an ad exec, the error is in your action, not in yourself.

Even when you're in charge, you can ask colleagues
for their opinions.

In the third year, each resident takes a month as head honcho, and this story is about that year—when *I* was in the role of medical consult. One of the things that medical consults do is run the codes: A patient goes into a cardiac arrest and you'll hear over the hospital loudspeaker, "Four one one—Airway Team." Everyone comes running. You start pounding the chest and shocking it with paddles to try to get the patient's heart to restart. Part of me was hoping that thirty days would go by and not a single coronary artery would clot, not a single lung would be blocked, and everyone would be healthy. Obviously, that didn't happen.

My first cardiac arrest was in the ICU, and as I started running there, I suddenly became very anxious. When you practice a code, you do it on mannequins; I'd never run a real code on a real patient. When I arrived, I took my place at the front of the bed where the medical consult stands—and then couldn't think of a single thing. My mind just went blank. Another resident started feeding me the facts: a sixty-one-year-old man had had a stroke and kidney failure and was now in respiratory arrest. As he talked, it was like my brain turned to soup and I couldn't remember a single protocol.

"Okay, begin chest compressions," I said, "and start bagging with oxygen." I remembered those two things. But what next? Did you shock first? Inject epinephrine? Adrenaline?

Someone pressed an electrocardiogram readout into my hands and I thought, "I hope this is going to solve the problem." But I suddenly couldn't remember a thing about reading EKGs.

When you read an EKG, you look for three things: a "P wave," a "QRS complex," and a "T wave." When a T wave looks like a tent instead of a camel's hump, that can be a sign of hyperkalemia—high potassium levels in the blood—which is life threatening. You have to give insulin, D50, and calcium immediately.

But I couldn't decide: Was this T wave really peaked? Sometimes you can have a pseudopeaked T wave, where the peaked T wave *doesn't* mean high potassium. What if I gave him the treatment and I was wrong? That could cause other serious problems.

I stood there debating with myself, frozen, too afraid to say anything.

Suddenly a new voice demanded, "Who is in charge here?" It was the cardiology fellow, barreling into the room. Fellowship is one step ahead of residency, so he was my superior. I said, "Me." Then there was an awkward moment, because we recognized each other and I could see that he was a little shocked. We had been friends back in medical school, but now he was ahead of me because I'd taken time off to do a PhD—and it was clear that if we *hadn't* been friends, he would have yelled at me for my incompetence.

He sidled over, looked at the EKG, said, "Hyperkalemia," and started barking orders. I thought, "Shit, I had it right!" Instead of being the captain of the ship, I'd cowered. Someone else had come and done it for me. If I had just said my first thought then I would have been the model take-charge resident and maybe saved this guy's life, but I'd been too afraid to say it, too afraid to be wrong. In the end, the patient did okay: they brought his pulse and blood pressure back by treating the hyperkalemia and then the code was over. But I just wanted to hide in a sea of white coats and slink off.

Of course, now I've run many codes, and if I'm not completely convinced of my first intuition I'll quickly say to someone, "Hey, here's what I think. Do you want to give me a second opinion?" Whether you're the medical consult or in any role in which you're deferred to as being in charge, there's no reason why you still can't seek support or advice, asking, "What are your thoughts?" You're almost never alone at the helm of a ship, or anywhere else, for that matter.

DANIELLE OFRI'S TIPS

▶ You don't have to feel the burden of "I must be 110 percent right on my first try, and I may not utter any evidence of hesitancy." Even the president of the company can turn to a trusted colleague and say, "What do you think? Here's my idea. Give me some feedback."

▶ You don't have to be the model of perfection to be good at your job. I'll never know all the medical facts the way a computer will, so I can say, "I don't know . . . but I'll try to find out," and still feel confident in my abilities.

▶ If you make a mistake, it's important to distinguish the action from the person. What you did was a mistake, but *you* aren't the mistake. Just own up to it and learn how you can do it better. Find someone you can trust to talk about it. And when you see someone else make an error, be that compassionate listener. Help the person acknowledge the error without shaming him or her.

JOANNA BARSH

"If you don't have a passion, there's nothing wrong with you. I think that life is not so much about following your passion, but about realizing that your journey is a long one. Focus on developing hard skills like problem solving, business writing, and presenting, and soft skills like taking initiative, getting along with others, and engaging in meetings. Get curious about what you enjoy doing (and don't enjoy), and notice what gives you a lot of energy."

Because of Joanna Barsh, there's an index card above my desk on which I've written the word "balance" with a line drawn through it. Barsh suggests replacing the idea of "work-life balance" with the concept of "managed disequilibrium" (a phrase she first heard from Google's Eileen Naughton) because no ambitious woman is ever going to feel that things are "in balance." Instead, we have to find what's meaningful to us and create conditions in which we can thrive.

A director emeritus at McKinsey & Company, Joanna Barsh has boundless wisdom, a great sense of humor, and a trove of data that she's used to develop her theory of "centered leadership." During in-depth interviews with over 165 men and women, she gathered data on thriving and rising at work; she then articulated her new (and almost shockingly sensible) model for thinking about leadership development in two books: *How Remarkable Women Lead* and the upcoming *Centered Leadership*. They should be required reading for every young person—man or woman.

Barsh is a strong advocate for women at McKinsey and beyond. She has been a New York City Commissioner on Women's Issues since 2002, appointed by Mayor Michael Bloomberg. She has also served the Partnership for New York City, the New York City Economic Development Corporation, the American Museum of Natural History, and the Manhattan Theatre Club. She has been a trustee of Sesame Workshop, the education organization responsible for *Sesame Street*, for eighteen years.

Barsh holds degrees from the University of Pennsylvania and the University of Chicago and an MBA from Harvard Business School.

Lessons I've Learned

If you're a creative person, know that some tasks require sticking with the facts.

My background was in art and literature, and after college I tried working in the movie business, then nearly became an English professor, and ended up in the management training program of the behemoth Macy's. I eventually realized that none of this was really for me, and soon afterward I applied to Harvard Business School. When I was admitted, it was as if I had to go—the feeling was similar to the one you get when there's a sale and you *must* buy something. Once I got there, everyone was talking about wanting to work in business consulting, and I was competitive enough to look into it.

A top firm hired me during the summer between my first and second years at Harvard; I think they were banking on the fact that I was this spunky young person and would bring some creativity to the work. But I really felt like I had tricked them into letting me in; I didn't have the strict business background of many of my peers.

And then I learned what I was going to be doing: I was charged with spending my days almost entirely alone (with the exception of the librarian) in the basement of a media company client—a dank, dark, miserable basement—and going through giant, heavy books filled with pages of data about ad revenue. I was supposed to figure out growth trends in order to change the economic outlook of this client. To do that, I would have to segment reams of data in some way that yielded insight. Finally, I was supposed to find a way to present the information so that my consulting firm would be able to help the client to strategize about going after new business. This was before the age of personal computers, so I spent my days laboriously copying the numbers out of the books and onto enormous sheets of accounting paper—I'm talking eight and a half by two feet each—in order to segment and add them up.

I felt anxious and overwhelmed. I remember sitting with these enormous sheets scribbled with numbers one night, alone in the office. It was really late. With about thirty sheets and hundreds of lines of data, it took over an hour to add each page, and nothing came out the same way twice. I began crying from fatigue and frustration, because I realized I was incompetent and did not know a better way to complete the task.

I finally solved this problem by using an algorithm, an equation I developed with a set of assumptions to try to represent the giant books of data. I remember thinking that it was not precise and could be wrong. Because I had looked at the trend data for days, if not weeks, I *knew* that some categories of advertising were growing and others were shrinking, some were large and others small—but when I drew the chart using my algorithm, it showed nothing. I knew it wouldn't provide the client with any insight. So what did I do? I literally fudged the numbers so that the chart looked right.

I did it in a marginal way—adding a point here, taking a half point away there, and voilà, it looked great! The tweaks adjusted the chart from meaninglessness to having an insight that I firmly believed to be true based on all the work I had done; it was just (I told myself) that I was a lousy mathematician. It put me in a kind of moral gray zone, but I was so naïve and so relieved to have come up with a solution for the client that I simply moved on.

My new and improved graph guided the client's resulting

revenue strategy—and the client loved it. I finished the summer feeling more confident and with a job offer. I went back for my final year at Harvard and lost sight of my summer.

But a few weeks later, I received a message on my answering machine: "Just trying to re-create your analysis," said a fellow from the firm. "The client loved it so much that they gave us another study, and I want to update it with the current numbers but I can't seem to re-create what you did."

I didn't call him back, and I didn't tell anybody what I'd done. I was filled with dread; I had nightmares; I couldn't focus on my work. I was burning with shame—it was as if I had killed somebody. I kept waiting for a call from the guy who'd offered to hire me, telling me that I was already fired. This went on for about two weeks, during which I received two or three more calls. Finally I called him back and said, "I can't find my analysis."

He responded, "That's okay. Just tell me how you did it." All I could say was, "I cannot remember without my notes!"

Now I felt like God had put his finger on me. My conscience would not let me rest. So I called up the guy who had recruited me and came clean, saying, "You probably don't want me to come back. But I'm going to tell you what I did and you can decide, because I can't live with this anymore—I can't live with the guilt."

After I told him, he started to laugh.

"First of all," he said, "I never want you to do that again." But he went on to say that he understood how I had gotten into the bind that I did without any instruction or supervision. He let me know that he would talk with his colleague—the one trying to re-create my analysis—and that I didn't have to worry about it. "Of course we don't want to rescind the offer," he said. "We do want you to come. I'm glad that you told me." Cue sigh of relief.

This very early mistake helped me in significant ways. First, it helped me to recognize my strengths and weaknesses. I understood that I could creatively problem-solve by seeing something differently or asking a question from a new perspective—but that I couldn't bring creativity to the analysis itself. Second, I became aware that in trying to belong at this company where I felt like I didn't really fit in, I'd reneged on my own sense of professional integrity—and that, in the end, my integrity was more important. Connecting with that helped me to develop a level of professionalism that I hadn't had before. Finally, I came to revere problem solving; even when there were no easy answers, I kept asking questions. Ironically, these high standards are what ultimately led to ascending up the company ladder and feeling at home in the world of consulting—"belonging" at the highest level. I became the partner who intuitively found the flaw in the model, the mistake in the spreadsheet, and the weak assumption. Over the course of my time in consulting, I became *known* as somebody who finds growth opportunities for media companies, proving that early mistakes can be fertile ground for honing particular skills.

*Another mistake was being more focused on my own
"good idea" than on the task at hand.*

Years later, I became a senior partner at my firm and was invited to a retreat with the other partners. We were tasked with thinking about the firm's direction. I love that kind of assignment so I went beyond the expected scope of the project, collecting videotaped interviews to present.

Well, I probably should have known that an eleven-minute video of talking heads raising criticism after criticism does not make for a great presentation, but that mistake was only the tip of the iceberg. I was invited to give my presentation to the most senior governance committee in the firm, and I called one of the firm's founders beforehand to tell him that my presentation would be about wanting the firm to go through a rebirth. I was basically proposing that we'd have an improved partnership between senior and younger people; that we would serve a broader set of clients, including more cutting-edge clients; and that we would create new positions for respected experts who would bring depth to what we do. His response: "You have a lot of courage." I didn't know what he meant, but I didn't think to ask.

The next day, we went into this big meeting at a fancy hotel in New York City. I'd never been invited to speak to this group before. These were "the big kids," about twenty older men, and they had a peculiar culture—for example, they sat in this giant U and when they wanted documents shredded, they would tear them up and throw their papers on the floor in the middle.

I came into this room and stood in front of the pile of ripped-up papers with two male colleagues. We showed our video and presented for a half hour. For the *next* half hour I listened to the group's sentiment, the gist of which was: *How dare you. We just elected you. Obviously we made a bad decision.* I tried to defend our ideas (and we had plenty of them) but they were so angry that I spent the entire time trying to stop myself from crying.

For a long time, I thought of this as just a terrible moment from which no lesson had emerged. Many years later, as I began to gather data on the development of very successful women leaders, and to create a model—"centered leadership"—to explain what the data showed, I realized a few important things.

When one of the firm's founders told me that I had "a lot of courage," I *knew* that was an odd thing to say. And part of me also knew there was something wrong with my plan, so I should have followed up to ask why he was saying that. I hadn't trusted my intuition.

I hadn't even been truly focused on my intent—what mattered to me—which was to think about where next to take this great company. The video *really* was eleven minutes of what we didn't like: "Here's something that's wrong, and here's another thing, and let me pile on another thing." These days, I would approach this kind of task through the lens of "appreciative inquiry," beginning with successes—and strengths—and building on that. If you want to bring your new ideas to the table and make changes, you must start by honoring what exists. That way, you release people's anxiety that you're going to kill what they're most trying to protect.

Finally, I hadn't prepared for a worst-case-scenario outcome, which was what I got; I couldn't even answer the group's questions because I was frozen with fear.

It took many years for me to see how much the firm believed in me to tolerate my doings. It took years, too, to learn the valuable lessons embedded in this horrible experience. Understanding those lessons affirmed my belief that mistakes are nearly always learning opportunities and that you should only call them "failures" if you *don't* learn.

JOANNA BARSH'S TIPS

▶ I've noticed that young people are often afraid of "living the wrong life." Every decision becomes momentous because they just haven't made many of them! They become afraid to decide anything, which can be a mistake in itself. Instead, start with what you really want to create and if the decision takes you a step forward, go for it. If you don't know what you want to create, focus on gaining a skill.

▶ Be open to stepping outside of your comfort zone. In our leadership trainings, we have a vocal coach who makes people sing in front of the group because it's a real experience of risk. Some people actually cry because they feel so ashamed, but once they do it and realize that they're still alive, that they're still breathing, they are stronger for it.

ALINA TUGEND

"I think we feel shame about so many things related to money. And we take it so personally. We're often not taught to balance our checkbooks or to negotiate our salaries, but we are expected to handle our money perfectly."

When Alina Tugend wrote a 2007 *New York Times* article about mistakes, she was flooded with grateful responses from readers and decided to follow up by writing a book—a terrific book—called *Better by Mistake: The Unexpected Benefits of Being Wrong*. Tugend says that the response to her article "made me realize that in a world where we're too often told that 'failure is not an option' most people—including myself— are hungry to hear that yes, we all make mistakes and that really is okay." The bestselling author Daniel Pink called her book "a fascinating and wide-ranging exploration of the deeply human phenomenon of screwing up."

Her book is also funny and approachable, lucid and intelligent, just like Alina was when we spoke over the phone about the mistakes she'd made in negotiating her salary over the years. She had so much good wisdom to share that I was actually able to put some of it immediately to use: when I talked with a friend who was putting off a difficult conversation with her boss, I passed along Alina's advice to begin the conversation via e-mail. This had never occurred to my friend, but she composed the e-mail and sent it off—to excellent effect!

A journalist for the past thirty years, Alina has worked in Washington, DC; southern California; London; and New York. Since 2005, she has written the biweekly ShortCuts column for the *New York Times* business section. In 2011, her personal finance columns received a Best in Business award from the Society of American Business Editors and Writers.

Lessons I've Learned

Even when you're grateful to have that first job, it's still a good idea to negotiate.

I've always wanted to be a journalist, and one of my first jobs was at the *Los Angeles Herald Examiner*. It was the late 1980s, and they offered me around two hundred dollars a week. I knew it was low, but I didn't negotiate because I was so glad to have a job—and as a young, single person I knew I could live off that puny amount.

After I'd been working as a reporter there for two years, I took on a role with the reporters' union. Suddenly I had access to a piece of paper that listed the salaries of all my colleagues. Reading that list was like a shock to the system; I discovered that I was being paid less than anyone else there. I had assumed we were all being paid a union rate according to seniority. In fact, many people were being paid over the established union rate. I felt betrayed—and foolish.

The newspaper wasn't doing well financially and I knew that it was unlikely I'd get a raise. Also, there was this fear in the back of my mind that maybe I wasn't worth more money. This, I've since learned, is a pretty common fear—especially for women—and one we have to work extra hard to overcome. In any case, the paper soon folded, but it was the beginning of a long learning curve about fighting for what I was worth.

By then, I was in my midtwenties, and the *Orange County Register* in California hired me. It was a larger and wealthier paper. The editor who hired me asked over the phone about salary. I threw out a number that was a little higher than what I'd been getting at the *Herald Examiner*. The editor laughed and said, "We can pay you more than that!" Of course, it's very rare for an employer to be that forthcoming and generous; it would have been good if I'd done some research to learn about the going rate! Even pre-Internet, I could have asked some close friends.

Learn to manage the emotions that come up during negotiations.

A couple of years after I began writing my column for the *New York Times*, my editor said, "You should ask for more money.

All the male columnists have." I had been so grateful to have the column in the first place that I hadn't thought to ask for more—and again, I was annoyed with myself. I'd built a successful career as a freelance journalist (often writing about business!) but somehow I still hadn't been able to master the business of negotiation. The whole endeavor made me uncomfortable, but I forced myself to ask the editor what *she* thought I should be making—and then I gritted my teeth and added fifty dollars. She helped me to compose an e-mail to the business editor. As I wrote it, I kept thinking that I was going to come off as greedy, as expecting too much and thinking I was better than I was. I was sure that he was going to say no.

But the business editor just said, "Fine."

It's not easy for either sex—except for those people who are born negotiators—to discuss salary, but women tend to personalize these things more than men. We have to try to know we're worth the money, be able to ask for it, and not feel crushed if it doesn't come through. Many factors go into an employer's decision about granting raises, and we need to understand that. But we also need to leave a place that undervalues and underpays us.

Do your research and don't get bogged down by missteps.

I don't think it's until very recently that I've been able to consistently negotiate when a number is proposed. When I got into my forties and fifties, with a successful freelance career, a *New York Times* column, and a published book, I began to speak up. If a magazine offered a dollar a word, I finally started to force myself to say, "Well, I usually make two."

I belong to a journalists' organization, which collects and publishes pay (anonymously) at various media outlets. I've had the experience of being offered $1.50 a word and then seeing that someone else is being paid $1.75 a word, so now I always do my research before the negotiation. I also just assume that an offer will come in somewhere in the middle, and that it's worth trying to hike it up. If you ask for $2.00, they might come in at $1.75. It may sound like a small difference, but it adds up.

But even recently, someone asked me to write a magazine article for a university magazine and asked, "What do you get paid?" Sometimes I get one dollar per word, sometimes two, depending on the publication, but I said, "About one fifty."

The woman hiring me said, "Fine." And right away, I thought, *Why didn't I ask for two?* I was kicking myself, because it would have meant getting paid another eight hundred dollars. And I realized, this is about the fear of overselling myself—like, "What if I'm not worth what I'm asking? I'd better *really* perform now."

So, knowing how to negotiate doesn't mean I always do it in the way I'd like to. But I'm getting better.

It never hurts to ask.

After reading my book, an editor contacted me and said, "We love your stuff. We'd like to pay you thirty cents a word to write for us." I was flattered, but I thought, "That's nothing." I didn't even think about asking them for more, because I assumed that if they were offering thirty cents a word, then they couldn't pay my normal rate. When I happened to mention this exchange to my husband, he pressed me to tell them—out of self-respect, and to make a point—that my going rate is significantly higher. Still, I didn't want to mention the money. I e-mailed back to say thank you and that I didn't have the time, but I threw in a line at the end: "I generally make quite a bit more than that." The editor e-mailed back saying "Okay, how about two dollars a word?" And so I went from thinking that this job wasn't even a possibility—to taking it.

It helps to understand that asking and talking about what we should get paid is problematic for most of us, and that the worst that can happen is getting a no. The conversation doesn't have to be so dramatic. It can be hard for women to say, "I think I'm worth more," or "Would you consider raising that?" because we worry that people will think we're full of ourselves. We worry that if we're given more money, it means we'll have to do everything perfectly. I have this friend who's a great journalist, and when she gets a raise, instead of feeling like, "Yahoo, I'm so happy and I deserve this," she immediately feels sick to her stomach. She feels she can't possibly be good enough to be worth the extra money. But we have to get over that mindset—it's one way we can work to close the wage gap between the genders for good.

ALINA TUGEND'S TIPS

► Asking for money can be easier over e-mail. As a journalist, I've learned that if you give someone a chance to get off the hook, they'll take it—on the phone it's easy to want to be nice, to say things like, "I know these are hard times and you probably can't pay this." (They'll probably say, "Yes, you're right.") I can be a little more hard-nosed by e-mail. You also have a written record of the conversation.

► If you do find yourself asking for money over the phone or in person, allow for silence right after you ask. It's a very powerful tool.

► Some key phrases I've used in negotiating are "I usually get x" or "I understand the standard rate is x." Then it's about business, and not about what you're worth or what you need. Never talk about what you "need," and never be apologetic.

► There's so much emotion attached to money that when you practice negotiating, you should think through not only what you're going to say but how you're going to *feel* in the face of pushback. And you have to come to terms with the fact that pushback doesn't mean you're wrong.

► You may have reasons for being willing to accept less money because you're getting something else out of the deal—like experience or prestige. But, especially these days, be very, very careful not to fall into the trap of working for free just for "exposure." In rare circumstances it can be worth it, but it's usually just exploitive. You're worth more than that. And exposure doesn't pay the bills.

SELENA REZVANI

"Sometimes in life, you are given options A or B and you want nonexistent option C. I wish I'd had the courage to overcome self-doubt earlier, to know that I didn't need a well-worn path to think something was viable as a career."

Selena Rezvani isn't your typical MBA leadership expert. First of all, she has a degree in social work, to which she attributes some of her skill in navigating tricky conversations and facilitating business meetings. Second, while she's ambitious and intellectually sharp, she also has a remarkably lovely way about her—when she speaks she is thoughtful, and her voice is calming. She's brought the breadth of her background and her considerable expertise to bear in writing two important books on women's leadership: *The Next Generation of Women Leaders: What You Need to Lead but Won't Learn in Business School* and *Pushback: How Smart Women Ask—and Stand Up—for What They Want.* As the same time, Rezvani created Women's Roadmap, which engages in women's leadership development and helps companies to create inclusive workplaces.

Rezvani has been quoted or featured in the *Wall Street Journal*, NBC, ABC, *ForbesWoman*, and *Jezebel*, and she writes a column on women and leadership for the *Washington Post*. For her work on this column, she won the Jane Cunningham Croly Award for Excellence in Journalism Covering Issues of Concern to Women in 2012.

She has a BS and an MSW from New York University and an MBA from Johns Hopkins, where she graduated first in her class.

Lessons I've Learned

The pressure to be a "good girl" can constrain you in every area of your life.

I grew up with a lot of good-girl-isms: don't ruffle feathers; don't be too direct or ask for too much because you could seem entitled or look demanding. These internalized "rules" followed me to college, where I noticed myself starting sentences in class with "This might be a silly idea . . ." or "I'm not an expert but . . ." Many of my female peers also took on this apologetic style, while male classmates seemed to confidently share half-baked, I-just-thought-of-this comments with ease.

Meanwhile, I lived with four female roommates and it was hard for us to communicate directly with each other because we feared confrontation: what would happen if we didn't express ourselves in just the right way? We worried about irreparably damaging our relationships if we were too clear about our needs, and so we did a lot of unnecessary apologizing. I never negotiated for what I wanted or advocated for myself. In fact, if I had a problem with one of my roommates, I would talk honestly about it *with everyone but that person*. This anxiety about speaking up also affected my budding professional endeavors. In my job at a university office, where some people weren't pulling their weight, I didn't want to say anything about it for the sake of keeping the status quo and the peace. Because of self-imposed constraints, I avoided tough conversations in every area of my life.

Pursue what you find most compelling, even if it means going against the grain or asserting yourself in new ways.

Even though I went right from college to graduate school in social work, I knew fairly quickly that traditional social work was not for me. While interning at a tough women's shelter in East New York, I built great relationships but never felt at home. I forced myself to do it anyway, thinking, "Don't be a quitter. You committed to this, you should stick with it." Meanwhile, I began to wonder about applying what I was learning to women in the workplace. After what I'd seen and experienced in high school and college, I wanted to empower women and help them to develop agency in their careers.

There was one problem: it sounded ridiculously unrealistic.

There was not a soul in my social work program doing anything like this. My peers wanted placements with the mentally ill and homeless, with teen mothers—and so a job with "working women" meant doing something like drug and alcohol counseling in an employee assistance program. I imagined that if I eschewed heavy-duty counseling for the corporate world, people would think I was defecting . . . and this stopped me cold. I was afraid of being criticized. Looking back, I wish I had had the courage to propose my out-of-the-box idea and campaign to move it forward—to simply ask!—because I would have gotten even more out of the program, and it might have helped someone else who wanted to do something similar.

After graduating, I took two different jobs: in one, I counseled HIV-positive individuals, and in another I worked with crime victims. It was like wearing a jacket that was either too small or three sizes too big—neither fit well, and both were uncomfortable. But even when my gut said, "No, no, no, no, no," I forced it. I wasn't conscious of it, but the fact that I thought I *had to* do traditional social work meant that I was still trying to be a "good girl."

And then one day a mentor asked me what I'd do if I had a magic wand, if there was no internal chatter saying, *You just spent all this money getting a degree so you're stuck with it.* I finally asked myself: *What do you really want?* What kept coming to me was that I would work with women who didn't feel empowered in their careers. I started a job search, thinking expansively, looking everywhere: Monster.com, my high school network, Craigslist, and more. On the day that I went to craigslist, I found a description of my dream job at a firm called the Great Place to Work Institute, which consulted to companies trying to create better workplaces for their employees. The description said "master's degree preferred"—and I *did* have a master's degree! So I applied. When I was offered the job of senior-level project manager, I took it, and this set the direction for the rest of my career.

Embrace challenges; usually, people don't expect you to do something perfectly right away.

I loved my new job because it was rewarding to give employees a voice; interestingly, I succeeded because of the valuable skills I'd learned at social work school. As I led focus groups and talked with managers at companies that were trying to create better work environments, I listened, read body language, and facilitated groups in an inclusive way. It just reinforced what I'd known all along—I'd been in the right program but with the wrong focus for *me*.

In 2006, I got married and my husband and I moved to Washington, DC. With three years of consulting behind me, I was able to find work at a similar firm, only now I was expected to present at conferences and to publish in magazines and journals that potential clients might read. During my first few public speaking stints, my knees were knocking and I forgot parts of my speech, but I faced my fear and it got easier over time. It was the same with writing and pitching articles to magazines; the first pieces I wrote were far from perfect. But each of these risks, whether small or more substantial, built my confidence. I became so emboldened that I pitched something to the *Wall Street Journal*—which felt like a big risk!—and, to my delight, they published it. When you have wins like that, you start to question what you've been doing your whole life—why have you been undermining yourself, insisting on perfection, and analyzing things to death before you act?

I started thinking about applying to business school so that I'd be able to speak the same language as people at these companies where I was working. As I applied for MBA programs, the familiar chants of self-doubt played in my head: *What if you fail? You don't have the math skills or the financial acumen. You didn't major in anything even related to business.* But I was accepted to Johns Hopkins and once I got there, I knew that I was going to drive this thing until the wheels fell off, to take it as far as it could go. There was no holding back now, no voice of doubt that could stop me.

And that relinquishing of fear was the most important moment of growth for me. I became unafraid to ask for what I wanted and to make bold suggestions. Even when I thought my professor might laugh in my face, I told her my craziest idea: Because senior-level executive women were like mythical creatures to me—I didn't know any, despite working with dozens of corporations—I wanted to find them and ask what advice they would give to a woman like me who was at the beginning of her career. I thought I'd do some interviews and put them into a book for one of my projects.

My professor didn't laugh—quite the opposite. She told me to go for it, and she said to think about my "dream team," the women I didn't even think I could get. Taking her advice, I compiled a list of very high-level executives, people like the CEO of the *Washington Post* and the chair of the Equal Employment Opportunity Commission. To my shock, many of them were willing to be interviewed. During these conversations, I learned so much that I thought maybe the project could help other women, and I pitched it to a publisher. It was published as *The Next Generation of Women Leaders*, and this set the next phase of my career in motion. As I spoke, presented, and led workshops in order to promote the book, the whole process emboldened me to do it for a living, and on my own terms. I was finally doing what I'd always wanted: helping to empower women in the workplace.

I opened lots of wrong doors before finding the right one because I didn't always listen to my gut. Eventually I realized that it has consistently been the best GPS for me in making career decisions. I would advise young women that you can put dreams on the shelf, but they will keep popping up, showing themselves to you and saying, "Hey, what about me? When are you going to give me attention?" Don't let self-imposed constraints or the idea that there's a certain kind of work you're "supposed to do" get in the way of taking risks and pursuing what you love.

SELENA REZVANI'S TIPS

▶ I didn't take advantage of social work school to pursue my *own* interests, but in business school I took ownership over my time and it was incredible. If you walk into graduate school with ambition and use the resources available to you, you can have a once-in-a-lifetime experience.

▶ You don't have to be a "math person" to thrive at business school. I worried that I'd never get into any program, but I was accepted to an excellent one and loved every minute of it.

▶ At school or at work, if you find yourself wishing for a new kind of policy or program, then ask for it. Make a good solid proposal. Go and invent the option you wish was there.

▶ Failing is sometimes the only way forward. You can read thousands of books about public speaking, but until you do it, you are not going to grow. Learning through experience is key.

CARLA HARRIS

"I often give speeches both internally at management firms and externally, and a question that comes up is, How do you stop focusing on the fact that you made a big mistake? People really struggle with that. So I give the listeners a framework: Stop and look at yourself. Did you learn something? Do you know what decisions or actions led to the mistake? You might realize that you need to be more active and present in your life, and in the decisions that you're making, because otherwise, life will happen to you."

During her freshman year at Harvard, an economics tutor told Carla Harris not to major in economics; she just didn't have the talent. Her response was to go straight to the freshman dean and sign up for economics as a concentration. Years later, one week before graduation, she went looking for that same tutor (who was still on campus, working toward his PhD) and found him in the library. "I just wanted to tell you," she said, "that I'm graduating next week, magna cum laude—in economics." She credits her parents for teaching her to "never count yourself out."

This attitude, along with her intelligence and drive, has

made Carla Harris one of the most successful and powerful people on Wall Street. She has provided investment and financial advice to corporations, public pension plans, foundations, and endowments during her tenure at Morgan Stanley, and she is responsible for enhancing revenue generation through client connectivity in her role as vice chairman and managing director there.

Harris has been recognized on numerous lists of influential people, including *Fortune*'s "Most Powerful Black Executives in Corporate America" and "The Most Influential List," and *Essence* magazine's "50 Women Who Are Shaping the World."

In addition to her financial career, she has a thriving career as a gospel singer and has put out three albums. She also wrote an excellent book, *Expect to Win: Proven Strategies for Success from a Wall Street Vet,* filled with advice that she calls "Carla's Pearls." Finally, she is deeply committed to philanthropic work that supports young people's education and development.

Lessons I've Learned

Don't be afraid to ask questions.

After graduating from Harvard Business School, I went to work on Wall Street because I was drawn to its fast pace and to the idea that I'd be using both my strong quantitative skills and my personal sense of judgment. I began my career as an investment banker in mergers and acquisitions at Morgan Stanley and never anticipated that I would still be there today as a full partner. Part of the reason that I love my job is that I'm able to bring my authentic self to the table—but that was something I had to learn to do over time. Early in my career, I didn't have an internal "mentor," although I learned a lot through my own continual self-assessment and drive to always improve. I also learned through feedback from colleagues, even when it wasn't tactfully offered. For example, it was reported to me that a senior person wondered if I was "smart or stupid" because she never heard my voice during meetings. I realized that I was submerging my authentic self, and after that I made it a point to always try to speak up.

I also learned through seeking new challenges as opportunities for growth, and a problem arose one time when I wasn't willing to ask a question related to one of those challenges. In this particular case, I had fought hard for an opportunity to do what's called "pricing a transaction." When a company is seeking to raise equity capital, it will hire an investment bank to market the stock, attract buyers, and then price the stock. We put together a road show, during which the company presents itself to potential shareholders and we figure out what the demand is going to be. After about eight days, we price the stock based on our understanding of the demand and market dynamics.

When you're pricing any deal, you not only allocate the

number of shares that are in the stated deal size; you add an additional 15 percent in case there's unforeseen selling pressure the day after shares have been priced—meaning in case your stock is not selling as well as you'd like. That way, you can buy that 15 percent back and actually help support the price. Going into a pricing deal, if you're not sure what the buying demand for the stock will be, you might even sell an *additional* 15 percent so that you could buy back a total of 30 percent if necessary, further supporting the price. This is called "going naked." However, you'd never go naked when you thought there was going to be a lot of aftermarket buying demand. If investors want the stock, they'll buy it, which will push the price *up*.

In this case, one of my first times pricing a transaction, I didn't really understand this, and I didn't want to expose myself as not knowing something. The guy who had priced the deal right before mine had "gone naked" and so I thought I needed to do the same. The problem was that he'd done it because he wasn't sure what the buying demand for the stock would be, and he needed to protect the price in the aftermarket. Alternatively, *my* deal was in stellar shape. I had demand for the stock that far exceeded the amount we were selling, and there was no need for me to "go naked."

I didn't yet understand these nuances. I sold extra shares of the stock and then watched as the price shot straight up once it was offered on the open market. This put my firm in a bad position because I had to *buy back* the stock at an increased price. It was a costly mistake and my firm lost money.

That day I learned that if you don't know, you need to ask. Often we don't want to ask for help because we don't want to be exposed as unknowledgeable, or we're afraid that somebody will reject us and not even give us the help. But if someone turns you down, just think, "Next!"—because somebody else *will* help you.

If you make a big, public mistake then own it in a big, public way.

I felt terrible about that mistake, and the guilt continued for many days. Meanwhile, a guy who worked at my bank decided to make a big deal about the fact that I'd made a mistake. He went around on the floor of our department, talking to my peers and colleagues, saying, "Wow, can you believe it! Oh, my gosh, we're *still* losing money on that transaction. Boy, that was really costly. I don't think I've seen anything like that in my career."

Finally, after a couple of weeks, I got tired of it and figured out a way to stop it. I took him into a room and said, "You've always been very supportive of me, and I know you want to see me do well. I just want to let you know that I understand the significance of this mistake; I learned from it, and I understand it was expensive. You don't need to keep talking about it and I'm sure I won't hear from you about it again, right?" That was the end of that. Sometimes a face-to-face conversation is the best way to defuse a difficult personality. If the person is trying to intimidate or bully you, the last thing you need to do is run and hide, because you increase their power. But if you stand up to it and say, "Hey, I see you," then most of the time, they evaporate.

I also learned that when everyone knows that you made a mistake, you need to make sure they *also* know you're taking responsibility. Your ownership has to be bigger than the deal that some colleague is making. I had gone to my boss behind closed doors and apologized, but I also should have been going to colleagues and peers on the floor, publicly joking and talking about myself, saying things like, "I can't believe I did that. If I didn't understand what it means to 'go naked,' I sure understand it now." Whenever there's a serious situation, humor can be an important tool. Don't use it to downplay what you did, but if you show that you can joke about yourself, your peers will respect you more often than not.

On Wall Street, things move quickly and I was soon assigned to another transaction that got priced the next week. I couldn't allow myself to be afraid that I might make the same mistake—and I knew I *wouldn't*. I'd learned my lesson: never again would I have a question and not ask somebody. Heck no.

CARLA HARRIS'S TIPS

▶ If you make a big mistake and everybody at work knows about it, then let people know that you learned from it and won't repeat it. That prevents other people from having leverage over you.

▶ Rarely is a mistake fatal. There's a recovery strategy for every single one, so the key is to ask yourself: How did I get here? What lesson did I learn? Then brush it off and move on, period.

▶ Women, more than men, tend to hold on to their mistakes—and it becomes like heavy baggage, creating a competitive disadvantage. There aren't enough people telling young women that mistakes aren't a big deal and that they need to set down that baggage.

▶ While I didn't have an internal mentor, early on I did have a sponsor. A sponsor is someone who is willing to advocate for you behind closed doors. He or she doesn't have to have a real personal relationship with you but does need to have a lot of respect for your work. Once I became one of the senior people who would go into a room and evaluate the junior people, I realized how subjective the process really is, which just confirmed my belief in the importance of having someone who will go to bat for you.

PART III

Learning to Say No

In his book *Working with Emotional Intelligence*, Daniel Goleman cites a major review of the data on male-female sex differences, one that reveals men "have as much latent ability for empathy, but less motivation to be empathic, than do women." While men are rewarded for being tough because it's macho, Goleman says, middle-class American women are brought up to be "emotionally sensitive" because it's seen as feminine. This dichotomy doesn't serve that group—or females in general—and it can resonate in screwed-up, infuriating ways at work. Sheryl Sandberg sums it up in her well-researched bestseller *Lean In*: "If a woman is competent, she does not seem nice enough. If a woman seems really nice, she is considered more nice than competent. Since people want to hire and promote those who are both competent *and* nice, this creates a huge stumbling block for women."

* * *

We're truly caught in a double bind: When does assertive become *aggressive*? At what point does being generous and helpful actually mean being *a pushover*? And what does all this mean for setting boundaries at work? "When women feel they can't say no," says Carrie Baker, a women and gender studies professor at Smith College, "they're often reacting to real interpersonal and structural barriers." On the flip side, the pressure to be "nice" and accommodating may mean that some women take on too much.

Interestingly, beyond office walls where women still do more caregiving than men, the opportunity to say no *because* of work can actually come as a relief. Anna Holmes, founding editor of Jezebel.com, told me that writing her first book was a revelation because she finally had an excuse to *not* be available to everyone in her life. "I think a lot of women probably feel this way," she said, "but I'd been socialized to be accommodating and to help other people—both family and friends. For the first time, I felt like I had an excuse to say no. No, I cannot talk to you on the phone. No, I cannot help you with that. No, I cannot go out to dinner. Just no, no, no, no. And it felt very freeing."

I thought of Holmes as I worked to complete this book— saying "no, no, no" in order to meet a deadline—and the result was that I felt the same way she did. It's liberating to "be selfish," as Holmes put it, to choose what's right for you because you must in order to complete a task. And I think of the power of "no" as I see students take on mounting responsibilities until they feel completely overwhelmed— and then dread backing out of any of them. Sometimes each of us has to prioritize, even if it means disappointing someone or quitting a commitment. In a society where we're expected to be busy all the time, where people tout their overwhelmedness as if it means they're winning at some crazy game, saying no can actually be a wonderful feeling.

The contributors in the following section say *no* to taking on more than they can possibly handle; *no* to internalizing the indifference of a bad supervisor; *no* to teenagers who push the limits; *no* to a meaningless job. If these experiences had been easy, they wouldn't make very good stories. Instead, they were difficult—and represented important turning points for each contributor. I hope that they'll give you the courage to say no when you need to.

ANNA HOLMES

"Someone had handed me this opportunity to make something that didn't exist before, and I really felt like it had to succeed. There was no option of failure because this was the first time that my name was going to be on the top of something. If someone said to me now, 'Do you want to create a website?' I would create a little more balance. With *Jezebel*, I only took care of the site—and not myself."

During a long conversation with Anna Holmes, which was interrupted by the fact that she had to take her very old cat to the vet, she was thoughtful, incisive, and completely without pretense. It makes sense that she was the founder of Jezebel.com, the blog for women that came on the scene in 2007 with a manifesto saying its editors "wanted to make the sort of women's magazine we'd want to read." It took off in ways that surpassed Holmes's or anyone else's expectations; with over a million readers visiting the site monthly, it became the go-to place for sharp and hilarious commentary on pop culture and media. *Salon* called it "a site whose success has offered one of the best examples of the heretofore dubious possibility that feminism, politics and high culture could effectively be mixed with pop culture, comedy and low culture."

Before founding *Jezebel*, Holmes worked at *Entertainment Weekly, Glamour, Star*, and *InStyle*. Her first book, *Hell Hath No Fury: Women's Letters from the End of the Affair*, was published in 2003. She left *Jezebel* in 2010. Since then, she has been working as a freelance writer and has developed and edited *The Book of Jezebel: An Illustrated Encyclopedia of Lady Things*, which was published in October 2013.

Lessons I've Learned

Whether you get promoted or not, whether you're part of the "cool kids club" or not—these things are not indicative of your worth.

After college, I was hired as an assistant to an editor at a popular entertainment magazine. I was excited to be with coworkers who talked intelligently and analytically about popular culture, and I enjoyed the sense of momentum that came with a weekly print deadline—of course, this was pre-Internet. My job was to open my boss's mail and answer her phone, but I was also given the chance to write and pitch story ideas. Every week, twelve "assistant types" would sit together for a pitch meeting with my boss, and initially it was a lot of fun to work in such a collaborative environment. Soon, though, it began to feel like high school. There was a lot of one-upping, as if all the assistants were competing with each other, and three "cool kids" who were my boss's favorites emerged from the pack. They'd shoot down or make fun of everyone else's pitches. Eventually, I think my enthusiasm and continual stream of ideas branded me as someone who wasn't as stylishly aloof as some of my coworkers.

One time, we were sitting around the table and I pitched an idea about the trend of screenplays (like Quentin Tarantino's *Pulp Fiction*) being published and sold as literature. My boss approved it. It was the first time she had given me the go-ahead to report and write a feature—before this, I'd done much shorter, front-of-the-book items. It meant a lot to me that I'd possibly have my name on a longer piece. I wrote a draft, and was of course open to making revisions, but she reviewed it and just said, "No, this isn't working." She didn't say why or offer advice about how to fix it. I thought it was good material, and of course I knew that the first draft wouldn't be perfect; still, she didn't seem to want to mentor or guide me. It was almost as if she found my energy and enthusiasm exhausting. Because I wasn't being embraced in the way I'd hoped for, I remember feeling vulnerable and disappointed, thinking, "Maybe there's something wrong with me. Maybe I'm not as sharp as I thought."

At the time, I was around twenty-one and my boss was thirty. Now I understand that thirty is pretty young—maybe she didn't know *how* to be a mentor. I've also come to realize that she was grappling with her own set of internal politics:

the magazine was run by men and it's possible that she thought she had to be like them, which meant not thinking too much about guiding young women. But I had no sense of that at the time. All I knew was that I believed my good work would be rewarded with a promotion, and eventually it became clear that it wouldn't be. For a few months, I sat in stunned semi-silence. I didn't know what to do with myself. I'd been there for two and a half years and it was almost like a love affair—I was devoted to one magazine and couldn't imagine doing anything else. I eventually had to come to terms with the fact that I wasn't getting recognized for my hard work and made the choice to leave that magazine to work for HBO.

I wish I could go back to the person I was at twenty-one and say, "You'll be fine. This is not the way every boss is. The way she's acting has nothing to do with your talent and potential." But it's difficult to see past things when you're in the middle of them, especially when you're working so hard that your job is nearly all you do.

Do take risks if it's financially feasible.

In 2006, I was working at *InStyle* magazine and was fairly content. I don't have much interest in fashion or in what celebrities wear, but the magazine wasn't offensive to me because we weren't instructing women on how to live their lives (as many women's magazines can). It was a very professional workplace, and I felt more like an adult and a respected colleague than I had in previous jobs.

One day, a blogger friend approached me because she'd been asked by Gawker Media to start something tentatively titled *The Girly Gawker*. She asked if I wanted to help with it, and I said no—but then spent two hours talking with her about what it could be. I'm glad that I was self-aware enough to think, "Okay, I *said* one thing but just *did* another. Maybe I am interested, and maybe I should think about this a little harder."

At around the same time, *InStyle* offered me a position running its website. Suddenly I had two opportunities: one for a stable company with good benefits and the other at Gawker, a new Internet company. It took me some time to weigh out the pros and cons. I had spent most of my early career not doing things that were risky because of financial constraints. It's easy for people to say "do something that scares you," but sometimes financial pressures aren't conducive to that. It can be paralyzing when you owe seventy thousand dollars in college loans and you know that late payments will lead to bad credit. Gawker seemed risky for financial reasons alone. It also didn't help that no one in my social circle was leaving print to work on a website. The Internet was still looked down upon as a lesser form of media. But when I thought about my career, I was afraid that I was going to spend the rest of my life captioning red carpet photographs and writing about things that bored me. The fear of inertia—careerwise—outweighed any fear I had of failing.

I agreed to do it, and two weeks later my friend decided that she was sick of New York and wanted to move back to London. She didn't want to work on the site anymore.

The people at Gawker said, "Okay, then, you're going to do it on your own." Suddenly my name was going to be on the top of this site—whether it succeeded or failed, that would be *on me.* I agreed to continue with the job on my own, not thinking, "I'm going to do a courageous thing," but thinking, "This is fucking scary."

I spent three or four months deciding what I wanted the site to be and interviewing writers. The design and name were worked out. I hired two people and we began test blogging just to get a feel for what the pace and voice would be like. I loved that time before the site went live; I felt like I was getting paid to sit around and imagine and plan. There was a certain amount of stress involved, but we weren't yet tethered to the news cycle. I could be contemplative and creative and not feel the pressure to bang out one post after another.

In May 2007, *Jezebel* was introduced to the world. It was terrifying and exciting, and within a month or so, it seemed like we were doing something right. Readership was growing and we were getting some press. For the first time in my career, I had autonomy: I could have ideas and execute them without running them through layers of management. I finally had a great conduit for all the energy that hadn't been appreciated at my very first job—and I got feedback and results that were directly tied to that energy and enthusiasm. If I worked hard, applied myself, and let my ideas run wild . . . the readers liked it. We got more traffic.

Part of the reason that *Jezebel* struck a chord was that we expressed genuine outrage about a number of things—not all related to pop culture. We were writing about the war on women and the war on abortion rights. We were writing about being fed up with "women's media." In fact, *Jezebel* wouldn't have existed without my years of feeling frustrated with the content I was being asked to produce at women's magazines.

And there was a lot of frustration bubbling under the surface. I remember one editor who had wanted me to write a feature called "What's Your Secret Sexual Personality?" She thought it would look good on the cover and so I'd had to make it all up, calling a "dream expert" and some psychologists. There was no reason for that story to exist, other than that she thought it would sell copies. Another time, the same magazine had wanted a sex story with "an Olympic theme"—this was around the time of the 2000 Olympics—and I'd had to invent vaguely athletic sex moves. I had done these kinds of soul-killing stories every month; pursuing any kind of critique would have just gotten me canned. With *Jezebel*, the critique *was* the story—a unique position that I relished.

Soon, hundreds of thousands of people were coming to the site. At one point, CNN did a screen grab of a comment made by a *Jezebel* reader, and I thought, "What? People at CNN are reading it?" I wanted to influence the cultural conversation on women in the media—and when it became clear that to some degree we were, it felt like a big responsibility.

I ran *Jezebel* for four years, and I saw that the harder I worked, the bigger the site got and the happier the readers and staffers were. In a way, *Jezebel* felt like more of a meritocracy than anything I'd ever worked on, and that's what was so seductive about it. I realized, "Okay, if I work at 110 percent, I get good results. If I work a little harder, I'll get even more out of it." But this success had personal repercussions: I never relaxed.

Take care of yourself.

Jezebel was more popular than I had ever anticipated. Eventually I was managing not only six staffers but also the expectations and personalities of millions of readers, some of whom were extremely vocal, demanding, and inconstant in their affections.

"Why aren't you posting about this?"

"I'm sick of reading about that!"

"How dare you take that opinion on this subject!"

Readers who were quick to express frustration and unlikely to express happiness were in the minority, but dealing with them started to wear me down. I didn't need to have my back stroked all the time, but we were expected to moderate comments and respond when possible, and this was exhausting, like a whole other job.

I was increasingly stressed. Not only was I posting once every ten minutes for twelve hours straight, but I also worked for the two and a half hours before we started posting and late into the night to prepare for the next day. At a monthly magazine, even if you're at your desk for twelve hours a day, you get up and go to lunch, you have a conversation with another editor or take a phone call—you do things that normal people do. But working in the way that I was, I burned myself out.

After I finally left, it took over a year to decompress. I found it hard to tear myself away from the computer and eventually realized that I was replicating my *Jezebel* lifestyle without getting paid for it. I started seeing friends, going out to lunch. I started exercising and taking care of my health. I had been addicted to the news cycle and the conversations that were going on, always afraid that I was going to miss something, but finally I realized that if it was important enough, I'd hear about it. It took a year until I was focusing more on myself than on what was happening on the Internet.

As rewarding as *Jezebel* was, I don't ever want to go back to that kind of lifestyle. With whatever I do next, I want both to feel a sense of ownership *and* to have some freedom. And I think that's an important message to drive home.

ANNA HOLMES'S TIPS

▶ It's not easy to do what you want, especially if you have student loans to pay or people to take care of, but if given the opportunity, try to challenge yourself. Try to choose the thing that's scary rather than what's expected.

▶ Don't let other people define who you are. When you're feeling unappreciated at work, just let yourself feel annoyed. Don't see it as a sign of worthlessness.

▶ Every woman can learn how to say no a little bit more in her personal life and also in her professional life, prioritizing herself and her own needs.

LUMA MUFLEH

"Whenever there's a form that says fill in your oc-
cupation, I put 'coach.' I don't put 'CEO' or 'executive.' And some people don't think 'coach' is a
respectable career. 'You went to Smith College and
you're a coach?' I am. And I've gotten to this place
because I was true to myself, but also because I
knew that I wasn't going to get it right away. I wasn't
going to figure this out at age twenty-two."

S itting with Luma Mufleh and talking about her work, you
can feel her passion for what she does, and her complete
lack of ego. Mufleh is the CEO of the Fugees Family, which is
a nonprofit devoted to child survivors of war. When she started
the Fugees in Clarkston, Georgia, it was a small operation that
gave refugee boys free access to organized soccer teams. As she
spent time with the boys, who came from places like Afghanistan, Bosnia, Congo, Iraq, Liberia, Somalia, and Sudan, she
saw them struggling to learn English as they coped with the
emotional aftermath of witnessing terrible things in their home
countries. She started to work with the children's parents, helping them with translation and eventually developing a business
called Fresh Start for America, a housecleaning cooperative for
refugee women. Now Fugees Family has grown to include

the first accredited independent school for refugees in the United States (Fugees Academy), as well as after-school tutoring, an academic enrichment summer camp, and soccer teams for eighty-seven girls and boys.

When I interviewed Mufleh, she was in Northampton, Massachusetts, to speak at a local private school, but she stopped at Smith College to talk to a small group over pizza. It was clear that her connection to the nonprofit was not confined to the organizational aspects of running it; she also had personal connections with the refugee children and their families. She told us that the last time she had been about to take a vacation, she'd made a joke to the kids that if they called her while she was away, she would charge them each a dollar. One of the kids was visibly upset and told her, "I know you're never coming back." Mufleh, who is so deeply aware of the lives of her students, realized that her offhanded comment wasn't a joke to this student—the idea of her leaving was frightening for someone who had lost family members in his home country. So she took off her watch—she doesn't go anywhere without it—and gave it to him, saying that he could keep it until she returned. "He still called me every day for the next week," she told us, "but I had to prove to him that I was going to show up, that I was going to follow through."

Lessons I've Learned

You might not always know your career path right off the bat—but have patience with yourself.

Growing up in a wealthy family in Jordan, I attended private school and rarely socialized with poor kids. I threw a birthday party every year and invited everyone in my class, and I remember this time when one of the few kids on scholarship told me he wasn't coming. I asked why and reassured him that I'd send my driver to get him. He didn't believe me, and he still refused to come—I think he didn't want me to find out what his life outside of school was like. This was my first glimpse of life outside of my own privileged existence.

After high school, I left Jordan to study at Smith College in the United States. My best friend at Smith was from a background that was the opposite of mine; in fact, she had grown up in a trailer. Everyone in our house wondered how this Jordanian "princess" and this first-generation student had hit it off so well, but we both had dysfunctional families and somehow had the same perspective on nearly everything. She taught me about life in a way that I would never have been able to learn in Jordan, because we would never have been in the same environment.

I had a wonderful experience in college, but when I graduated, I didn't have a sense of what I wanted to do. I knew that I didn't want to go home—but that was all I knew. Everyone else was getting a graduate degree or going to law school or working on Wall Street, but I needed some time to figure out what should come next. I think a lot of what we want is shaped by our parents' and our peers' expectations, and so you go from kindergarten through college without pausing to ask, what do *I* want? And I needed time to consider that.

I hit rock bottom pretty quickly because of some issues with my family. I was determined to stay in the United States but my papers hadn't all come through. I moved to Atlanta because the weather reminded me of home, and I worked in restaurants. I wouldn't go to any alumnae events because I was ashamed to say, "I'm a waitress."

I soon started volunteering as a coach for a girls' soccer team at the local YMCA. Although it was enjoyable, I became frustrated with the overly competitive nature of youth soccer. During this time, I'd often drive to neighboring Clarkston, where there was a Middle Eastern grocery store that sold foods that reminded me of home. One day, after missing my turn, I found myself driving by an apartment complex and saw some kids playing pickup soccer. The way they played—barefoot, with a makeshift ball and no goal—reminded me of the soccer I'd grown up with in Jordan. It affected me. I went back the next day, this time armed with a soccer ball. Little by little, we got to know each other. They were refugees from war-torn countries in Africa, Asia, the Middle East. They didn't speak much English, but they all loved soccer. I became their coach. We named ourselves "Fugees," short for "refugees."

The Fugees began as one team but quickly became two and

then three. Siblings would come and say, "Coach, I wanna be a Fugee," and so we grew. Some seasons we had cleats; others we'd be scrambling to find them. Some days we'd get kicked off the field or locked out. I was tutoring the kids but we had no space to study, so we used headlights from my car in the park, or flashlights in the hallways of their apartment buildings.

Meanwhile, I learned about these kids' educational and home lives. Often, their parents made minimum wage and would literally run out of food by the end of the month. At school, they were set up for failure from day one, put in "age-appropriate" classes even though they'd had no formal schooling. They were expected to take algebra although they couldn't add, to study Shakespeare even when they couldn't read. The kids got passed through the system so that they wouldn't be a burden—and for the longest time I saw this and did nothing. But at a certain point, when I'd spent enough time with them, these kids and their families became my own. I finally knew that even though I didn't have a plan, the substandard soccer fields and used cleats were no longer acceptable. The lack of accountability and support in the school system was unacceptable.

I met with the parents of some of my players and presented them with an idea: I would raise funds to hire a teacher who could give their kids more individualized instruction, allowing them to bridge the gaps and truly learn something. The parents of six students were willing to take a leap, and in the fall of 2007 the Fugees Academy began. Each year the school has grown, and it is now the first accredited independent

school for refugees in the United States. It operates out of two
floors of rented church space and serves a co-ed student body
of eighty-seven middle and high schoolers. Fund-raising is a
big part of what I do, but I also serve as principal, teacher, and
head coach. The year-round programming runs from sixth
through tenth grade, and we'll graduate our first class of se-
niors in 2016.

All kids at the school play soccer on our teams, and I tell
them that they need to be engaged physically, mentally, and
emotionally in both academics and on the field. "We care about
you," I tell them on opening day every year. "We will ask a lot
of you, but we are also giving a lot. We see each one of you as
capable of growing, of succeeding. But that won't happen unless you are willing to work for it. And that's why the standards
here are high, it's why we're hard on you—because we believe
in you." This seems to really make an impact. I don't think kids
ever hear that their school cares about them.

I've always been the person with the vision for the school,
but to make it actually happen, I've needed to recruit people
who are much more organized and extroverted than I am.
Surrounding myself with colleagues who are totally unlike me
makes me stronger. What I love—and what I think is my real
strength—is coaching and being with the kids. When my
board wants to send me out on the road to fund-raise, I often
tell them that I can't speak about our mission and our work if
I don't spend most of my time out on the field coaching or doing things like having dinner in kids' homes. And the kids

always need to know they are more important than any award
or any recognition that our school gets.

I'm always pushing our teachers: How can we create an
environment where everyone feels capable? If a kid is struggling, what can we do better? Does he need one-on-one attention? Additional services? We discuss each and every kid—the
details of his or her home life, academic life, athletic life. We
ask ourselves: where can we help each kid feel confident? If
they start feeling confident in one area, it affects all the other
areas. We still have failures with kids. Failures within the organization are hard to recover from—but failures with the
kids are harder.

*Be mindful of when a kid's story resonates with you,
and of the ways in which this might affect your
behavior.*

One mistake in my career path that really stands out has to do
with my treatment of a student named Duke, who was probably the most gifted soccer player I ever coached. He wasn't
arrogant about his skills; he was very humble. He took care of
the weaker players. I remember games where he could have
scored three or four goals but would set up for the weaker
players to score. He was very much a team player, and as a
coach, I always appreciated it.

Duke was fifteen and had come to Clarkston with his

twenty-two-year-old brother after their parents had been killed in the Liberian war. I felt for him, maybe because in a way I'd also lost my parents—they were thousands of miles away and barely spoke to me—and I very quickly established a different set of standards for him than I had for the other kids.

Duke struggled academically. When he arrived in America, he didn't know how to read or write and I took a personal interest in seeing that change. I'd go to his house and literally drag him out of bed and take him to school. I also told him he needed to come to tutoring every night—but he didn't want to show up for tutoring in front of the rest of the team. "It would actually be beneficial for them to see a weakness in you," I told him, and when he still refused I said, "I'll tutor you privately, or I'll bring someone to do it at the library." Still he wouldn't come.

At home, no one took care of him; it was just three boys living together, each fending for himself. I was struck by that. And so if he said that he was hungry, I would go and buy him groceries or take him to McDonald's. On the field, I would make excuses for him. If he showed up late, he would still get to practice; other tardy kids would have to run laps the whole time. Normally if kids skip practice altogether, they don't get to play in games—but he did. In a way, I was treating him like a victim, and I think a lot of people who work with vulnerable kids, kids who have had hard lives, do the same thing. We make excuses for them and it's damaging.

One day I was talking to another kid on the team who

happened to be failing all his classes. I was ripping into him, saying he had to get it together or he wouldn't be able to play, and he said, "What, I'm not Duke? I can never be Duke for you."

The statement stopped me short. He thought he was lesser than Duke in my eyes. It was like a slap in the face. I thought to myself, What am I doing? I'm not being fair to the rest of these kids. I realized that having treated Duke differently from the others made the team weaker; I had to change my attitude and set appropriate boundaries for him, just as I did with my other students.

By that point, Duke wasn't going to school regularly. He was failing half his classes. He couldn't read, but he got by on his charm and athleticism. Finally I cracked down, but still he thought he could talk his way out of it. It took a year, but eventually I had to let him go. Once he was gone, kids saw that their coach meant what she said—that they needed to go to school, to show up on time for practices and games. And so the team and the program became a lot stronger.

At the same time, it's still something that makes me sad to think about. Duke ended up dropping out of school six months after he was kicked out of the program, and he's fathered three children at a young age. I saw the goodness in him, like you do with all kids, and I wanted it to come out. Part of me thinks I could have changed him. If I'd toed the line, maybe he would have buckled down and learned to read; maybe he would have succeeded academically and developed self-respect. But part of me knows that only he could have changed his trajectory.

I have had gifted athletes since then, but they were not treated the way Duke was. No excuses. I'm quicker at making decisions to kick players off the team. Kids get warnings, but the third time—that's it. And since my mistake with Duke, I've had to give fewer warnings because kids think, "If she can do that with *him*, then there's really no coddling around here." In fact, they all know the story or a version of it, because I'll tell them from the beginning: "I had this really gifted player, I bent the rules for him, and he never made it. It wasn't that *he* made the mistakes—*I* did." And I tell them, "I'm not going to again, so don't push me."

Sometime later, another incredibly talented player joined the team, a kid who also struggled academically, and I grabbed him into our school right away. When he showed up late one day to practice along with three other kids, I had them all run *the entire time.* Never again in four years on the team did those kids show up late. Setting a limit like that might be the hardest thing that you do—but you have to do it because then the kids know you're holding them to a standard.

Remember what got you here in the first place.

Fugees Academy continues to raise quite a bit of money and has grown exponentially in recent years, but we still have failures. During the same week, I had a potential big donor cancel a meeting and I came very close to being on *Oprah* but didn't make it. It was like a roller coaster, and on the drive home from New York I started crying. It's a huge responsibility to feel like, "If we don't raise this money, what's going to happen to the kids?" And it's personal, because I know them. They're not numbers—I'm not fund-raising for students one through fifty-eight. No. I'm fund-raising for Obi and Bob and Takoshi and Yaka and Fatu. It's hard when you hear people say, "Not this year. I'm giving to my kids' private school." You bite your tongue so that you don't say, "Your kids' private school does not need money. They have a $120 million endowment. You need to give to us."

I get told "no" over and over again: "We're not going to fund this" or "That isn't possible" or "Why are you doing this? There is no way it's sustainable." Some days I'll think to myself, it would be much easier to get a job in marketing or something else that I wouldn't have to worry about, something less stressful. But in those moments, I think of the kids. When they first come in, a lot of them say they want to be professional soccer players, doctors, and lawyers, but some are starting to say they want to be teachers—and I think my work will be done when one of them can take over the school.

Getting to what I now understand to be "my work" took time (years of uncertainty, really) and tenacity. I would advise young people to think imaginatively about where an interest—in my case, soccer—might lead, and to be open-minded about the ways in which you might make your contribution to the world.

LUMA MUFLEH'S TIPS

▶ The burnout rate in nonprofits is five years, so you have to carve out time for yourself and be really protective of it. I meditate for at least twenty minutes every day and take long bike rides on the weekends.

▶ I didn't have a specific path after college, but a lot of my friends did. They worked on Wall Street or got their PhDs, got married, and had kids. Now in their late thirties, many are going through career crises. I didn't do any of that and I am very happy at the point where I am. I struggled earlier. You have to realize that at some point you'll struggle.

▶ When you get the alumni quarterly and you read about your friends who are PhDs or MacArthur fellows or Rhodes scholars, have a shot for each one and keep a good sense of humor. Life is about doing what you love.

▶ We need to be able to take criticism and use it to improve ourselves. In sports, coaches have that approach; they'll just say directly, "I need you to do this."

RUTH REICHL

"There's a trade-off you have in your life, always, between time and money."

It's hard to explain what it's like to read Ruth Reichl's critically acclaimed, bestselling memoirs. In addition to telling completely engaging, funny, and moving stories about both her life and the development of her career as a writer and food critic, these books are each their own sensory experience. They include sumptuous tales of meals she's eaten and recipes she's invented, including many that have become some of my absolute favorites. (Take, for example, the following: an entire pumpkin with the seeds taken out, stuffed with bread and Gruyère cheese, white wine, and cream, its top popped back on so it can be baked in the oven. This insanely good concoction is called Swiss Pumpkin, if you want to look it up.)

When she was just twenty-two, Ruth Reichl published her first cookbook, *Mmmmm: A Feastiary*. She was soon hired to become a food writer and editor at *New West* magazine. From there, she went to the *Los Angeles Times*; below, she tells the story of becoming its food critic. In 1993 she was recruited to the *New York Times*, and later to *Gourmet* magazine, where she served as editor in chief for ten years. Currently, Reichl is a producer on the movie that Fox 2000 plans to make from one of her bestselling memoirs, *Garlic and Sapphires*, which is about her days reviewing restaurants in New York City (which she usually did in disguise so that staff and chefs wouldn't recognize her!). Her first novel, *Delicious*, will be published in 2014.

Ms. Reichl has won six James Beard Awards and numerous awards from the Association of Food Journalists. She has an MA in art history from the University of Michigan.

Lessons I've Learned

It's very tempting to settle for security.

When my first husband and I moved to San Francisco in the early 1970s, we lived in a communal house to save money so that we could take turns devoting time to what we really loved. For the first six months, Doug did carpentry to support us, and I wrote. Then it was my turn to work so he could make art, and I went to a temp agency to look for a position. I had previously worked as a book designer (which, admittedly, I was not very good at), and though I didn't love the work, it helped me find an open position. Wells Fargo Bank hired me to design the employee newsletter.

This was before the age of computers, and I had to use rubber cement to literally glue the text onto boards to be photographed. It required steady, nimble fingers and good eye-hand coordination, of which I had little. I was so bad at getting the lines straight, in fact, that I would have to sneak the boards home at night and get Doug to do it. But the rest of the job was easy, and they were paying me a lot of money. I was in my early twenties and it felt good to have a response to the question "What do you do?" I didn't really know what I *wanted* to do with my life (although I had a vague notion that I wanted to be a writer), and it seemed that when I was in the office, it was the answer to all my problems. I got into the flow of it and wasn't really conscious of how much I didn't like it.

Because actually, I was surrounded by people I couldn't stand. I had this fantasy of being part of the office group, and there is a kind of seduction that happens—you go out to lunch with people and if you're personable, you make "friends," but it's dissatisfying when you walk away and think, "These are not people I would ever choose to spend my time with." My colleagues were all very different from me, in terms of temperament and lifestyle. And there I was, living in a commune in Berkeley, getting on a bus every morning to go over to San Francisco and then coming back every night, feeling such a sense of disconnect between my home life and the world of this office. We lived in a very loose household, and I had get to work by eight o'clock, which meant leaving at six in the morning to get the bus. I would be up at five thirty and sometimes my housemates would still be sitting with a bottle of wine and talking, having stayed up all night. I'd be going off to work—thinking, "Grrr! Another early morning!"—and they'd be having these deep, interesting conversations. Then I'd get home late because of the long commute, and everyone would be having a good time as I walked in in my office clothes, feeling angry.

At the end of the three-month temp period, Wells Fargo offered me a full-time job at what to me was an enormous salary—and without hesitation, I accepted it. I went home jubilant and said to Doug, "I've got a job! We're going to be making so much money!" He looked at me and said, "Are you out of your mind? You hate it! You're so grumpy every morning when you go off! Don't do this. Go in and tell them that you're out of there. Do not take this job."

His words stopped me cold. He was right: I had accepted a job that I truly hated. But it's really hard to say no to security and to a prestigious position, and if I hadn't been married to this very nice man who shook me and said, "This isn't what you want—stop it," I know I would have done it.

I went in and quit the next day. "Not only am I not taking this job," I said, "but this is going to be my last day." It was like my heart was singing; I was so elated to be out of there.

That was the moment when I decided, "From now on, I am going to enjoy my jobs. I am not going to do work I don't like." Right afterward, I went to work at a restaurant called the Swallow in the university art museum in Berkeley. It was run as a collective, and you had to work for free during the first couple of months as your "investment." We made all our food from scratch, and everybody helped with all parts of the process. That kind of work uses both your physical and mental energy—you get *really* tired. But you're also thinking all the time: "How can I make this dish better?" and "Oh, my God, we're running out of food, we've got to go back and make more food. How can we do that with what we have?" I loved the people I was working with, loved interacting with the public—everything about it was fun for me. Even the monotonous work, like doing the dishes, was entertaining: "How fast can we do these dishes? Let's see if we can do this faster than any other group!" It was long hours, we didn't make much money, and I would come home exhausted, but it was a thousand times better than coming home from my previous job because I actually loved what I was doing.

And ultimately it led to my career as a restaurant critic. While I was working at the Swallow, I also started doing some freelance writing for local magazines. One of my editors at *New West* magazine used to eat dinner at the restaurant a few nights a week. One night he stopped me and said, "You know, you're a much better writer than our restaurant critic. And you can cook. Have you ever thought about writing restaurant reviews?"

Frankly, it had never occurred to me to think of it as a legitimate career move; the first thought I had was: *Free meals!* Doug and I were so poor—I didn't even have a credit card and we never went out to eat—so for that reason alone, it seemed like a fantastic opportunity. So I said, "Sure. Try me." They

sent me out for two trial meals, I wrote them up, they fired
their restaurant critic, and my life was changed forever. I wrote
for *New West* for six years, and then the *Los Angeles Times*
hired me to be its restaurant critic. I had never, ever imagined
my life taking that particular turn.

*Doing work that you love can inspire others
to do the same.*

I went to work as a restaurant critic at the *Los Angeles Times* in
1984, and I was always complaining about the paper's terrible
food section. After about three years, the editor came to me and
said, "Okay, I'm tired of listening to you complain, I'm giving
you the section." At that time it was the largest food section in
the country, about sixty pages every week. It had a staff of
twelve and a kitchen and a photo studio. After some hesitation,
I ended up taking it over. From the moment I started, the managing editor (who had been working on the section for twenty
years) hated me. *Hated* me. She felt an allegiance to her old
boss—who had just retired—and we did not see eye to eye on
anything. But she was very good at making things run on time,
so I kept her on.

After a while she got to know that although we had nothing in common, I admired and depended on her because she
was hardworking and did her job really well. We grew to a
place of mutual affection despite our early differences. I would

tell her stories from my past: "Oh, back in Berkeley, my husband and I lived on nothing." I would talk about what a great period that had been because I'd given myself the time to figure out what exactly I wanted—and more importantly what I didn't want—out of life.

Apparently this made an impact on her, because after a year of working with me, she approached me and said, "I'm quitting. I don't want you to think it's because I don't like you; you're the best boss I've ever had. But knowing you, and hearing your story, made me realize that I have never taken a chance on anything. I look down the road and I can see myself here at sixty-five. But my husband and I have broken up, I have no responsibilities right now, so I am getting in my car to drive around the country until I find out where I want to live. I'm going to do what you did when you were a kid because if I don't take a chance now, I'm never going to do it." And she went off and ended up living in Portland, Oregon. She found a new person to marry, and she wrote me a note and said, "Thank you."

She had always worked in a safe job, and I think she just hadn't known who she was or what she wanted—maybe she had never even thought about it. I understood how easy it is to fall into that place, because I almost did the same thing when I was working at Wells Fargo. But as a young person, I had ultimately been willing to trade money for time. Your best investment is yourself, so it seems to me that it's important for people to have *some* period in their lives when they get to just listen to themselves, and to figure out every day what they're going to do.

RUTH REICHL'S TIPS

► Get the broadest education you can. You will never again have a chance to study the way you do when you're in college and graduate school, so don't focus too completely on one subject. You may discover a passion you didn't know you had. And knowing a lot about art, literature, science . . . down the road, it will serve you well.

► Don't expect too much of yourself when you're young. It's better to be a late bloomer than an early one; so many young successes flame out and spend the rest of their lives lamenting what they used to have.

SHARON POMERANTZ

"How were you supposed to look for work, or get a resume together, when you had few weekends or holidays off, little savings to lean back on, and were battered by exhaustion and terrified of your own shadow?"

"My parents said, 'You can be anything you want, as long as you can support yourself,'" says the novelist Sharon Pomerantz. After graduating from Smith College in the early eighties, what Pomerantz really wanted to be was a writer, and she happened to choose one of the most expensive cities in which to try out her dream. As it turned out, one of the jobs she took as a struggling recent grad—shining shoes on Wall Street—would be one of her most rewarding. It was this experience that gave her the idea for her wonderful first novel, *Rich Boy*. It tells the story of a Jewish boy from Philadelphia who—like Pomerantz herself—becomes the first in his family to attend college. A driven young man, he has no one to show him how to thrive in the educated, moneyed world he has entered (only a wealthy roommate who throws away his shirts and buys new ones instead of doing the laundry) and he has no road maps as he eventually navigates life in the highest strata of Manhattan society.

Rich Boy won the Foundation for Jewish Culture's Gold-berg Prize for Outstanding Debut Fiction (a National Jewish Book Award); it was chosen by *Entertainment Weekly* as one of the Ten Best Novels of 2010 and by *Booklist* as one of the Ten Best First Novels of 2010. Pomerantz's short fiction has appeared in numerous literary journals, as well as on NPR's *Selected Shorts* program, and her story "Ghost Knife" was included in *Best American Short Stories 2003*. She teaches writing at the University of Michigan.

Lessons I've Learned

Consider trusting your instincts—even if they're telling you to quit when you've barely begun.

The worst job I ever had was also my first job in New York. I landed there with only five hundred dollars and the promise of a friend's couch to sleep on, and was soon hired to work as a reporter for a community newspaper on Long Island. Let's call it "The *Post*." The salary wasn't great—$325 a week, no benefits— but it was a steady paycheck. I was living in Brooklyn (this was 1989, when Brooklyn was still cheap) and didn't understand how far Brooklyn could be from Long Island, depending on where you lived.

On my first day of work, the commute took nearly two

hours. My anxiety mounted as I rode the F subway line to the A, then made two changes on Long Island Railroad, then speed-walked, sweating, to the paper's cramped offices located over a strip of shops on an expensive suburban block in Long Island. I arrived harried, confused, and late. A tiny, hunchbacked receptionist was screaming into the phone, but she paused long enough to order me to hurry down the hall. In front of the office marked "Managing Editor," a policeman was handcuffing a man around my age; the man was staring at the ground, looking deeply ashamed. I never did learn what happened to the man in handcuffs, but the incident set the stage for one of the more interesting jobs of my career.

The managing editor, Jason, introduced himself and jumped right to business. He launched straight into telling me about the stories I'd be working on, including one that afternoon: I was to interview a newly elected community leader. I had expected to have things explained to me, sort of like I was an apprentice, but that was not the case. I was excited but also terrified that I simply had to learn by doing.

Just then, as if on cue, the publisher of the paper emerged from his office and joined us. Carl was a man of average height, in his late thirties, with a long face and close-set eyes. He gave off an air of authority combined with a homely vulnerability that I later learned could turn quickly to rage. It was Tuesday, he said, and I should expect to be working well into the evening, since Tuesdays were late nights. (So were Mondays and Wednesdays, but he didn't say that.) Then he took out an enormous wad of cash and asked, "You need money to get you to payday?" Not waiting for a response, he peeled off three twenties and put them on the table next to me, then walked away. There was nothing to do but take the money, which I could certainly use, but he'd been unclear on whether it was a gift or an advance on my salary or why, exactly, he'd decided to hand it to me before I even started working. Did I really look that down-and-out? Was he just trying to get off on a good foot, or make me grateful and beholden? I'd soon find out.

Most sane people would have walked away from this place (and plenty had), but this never occurred to me. I wanted an entry-level journalism job, and they were hard to get under the best of circumstances, let alone during a recession. I could have waitressed or babysat and continued looking for something better, but I'd been working since I was twelve and had already been a nanny, a bartender, and a shoe shiner; I'd cleaned rooms, washed dishes, shelved books, and refinished furniture. When you're from a blue-collar family, you don't see the romance in blue-collar work. I had a college degree, and I wanted to use it, and I wanted my parents to see me use it, so I stayed—and was immediately overwhelmed.

Four stories a week, I would learn, is a lot of stories. For the first eight months I worked there, I was the only full-time reporter. I had worked on my high school newspaper, and had done a few op-eds for my college newspaper, but I'd never researched and written a serious news story. I was thrown right into the pool, anxiously trying to make sense of the barrage of new facts as I researched a congressional reaction piece, calling members of Congress to ask them about proposed changes to the foreign aid budget.

Researched articles on foreign policy are generally beyond the purview of a community newspaper, because you can't cover local, national, and international news with a tiny staff unless you drive them compulsively. Carl was fond of telling all his employees about his widowed mother who'd raised two children while working at a bank. In over thirty years on the job, she was never late, never took a sick day, and when she had to phone home, she waited until her break and went to the pay-phone on the corner so as not to cost her employer the price of a local call. This was the level of loyalty and thrift he expected from everyone who walked in the door. The paper wasn't a job for Carl, it was a religion, a way of life.

When we were on deadline, Tuesday nights, Jason and I would be up until one a.m. doing a meticulous read-through on the long scrolls of prose pulled out of the typesetting machines. My eyes would hurt and everything would start to run together; I knew I was missing things and then would spend days in terror. If even the tiniest of corrections was missed, Carl became apoplectic and would be on the lookout for someone to blame. I rarely experienced Carl's wrath directly because he didn't tend to yell at women, only at men, so when he was angry at me, he let Jason relay the message.

For most of that year, I had no weekends off. Saturdays I did phone interviews (this was before cell phones, when you had to wait around all day to get a call returned). Sundays I covered events. Holidays were work time, except Thanksgiving (because it always fell on a Thursday). Christmas week the paper closed, but I had to use some of that time to catch up on stories, and when I came into the office, others were there as well. The *Post* allowed no sick time, and only when I'd fainted in the office from a high fever was I allowed to leave and go to a doctor (luckily this happened on a Wednesday, after we'd put the paper to bed). I had no social life, I rarely saw my family, and, from lack of sleep and the pressure at work, I put on ten pounds and broke out in hives all over. Since I didn't have any time to shop for clothing, almost nothing fit me. I've never looked worse than I did that year, at age twenty-four—not exactly the glamorous city life I'd dreamed of.

You'd think when I got home each night, I simply collapsed from exhaustion, but sometimes, even at one or two a.m., I was too amped up on adrenaline and caffeine to sleep. Those moments were when I took out my journal and wrote, indulging in my one true passion—fiction. I wrote the openings of short stories I hoped to complete someday, fragments of scenes, bits of dialogue, and character sketches.

Be brave enough to define your own future, rather than letting a bad job define you.

Many writers had passed through the offices of the *Post*. On the few occasions when I attended press events, other reporters would gather around me and shake their heads, pat my shoulder, and tell me it would be okay. One particularly late Tuesday night, the phone rang in the offices and I picked up. A voice on the other end knew my name. "I used to work there," he whispered. "I know how you feel. And I heard about a job opening." This happened twice, which was puzzling. Later I found out this wasn't so unusual. People who worked for Carl helped others to leave, crafting a kind of underground railroad for young reporters.

I stuck it out for another two months, and then I saw an opportunity. My roommate was working in a school, and one day she came home with lice. Pretty soon, we were infested. We spent a day burning, washing, and otherwise scrubbing our apartment, and when I called in to work, it occurred to me that maybe Carl, for once, would tell me to stay home. After all, his kids came to the office, and even he would not want to risk an infestation. This was exactly what happened—and suddenly I had four days off to look for a job that had everything the *Post* didn't. By the end of my time out of the office, I had a resume and several cover letters; a week later I had interviews; and by mid-July, I had a job doing PR for a nonprofit in Manhattan. This felt like a miracle because unemployment was high in 1990, and because it was a writing job that would give me more weekends off (and some vacation time), raise my salary, and shorten my commute.

Everyone was shocked when I gave notice. Having made it almost a year, I don't think they expected me to leave (or maybe they didn't think anyone would hire me). Carl took this as an opportunity to point out, not for the first time, that I had no talent. He said, "You'll never amount to much as a writer." I didn't respond, only stood up and walked out of his office. If I hadn't distinguished myself at the *Post*, I had survived, and for now that would have to be enough.

After I could calm down and settle into my next job, I began to see how I had actually managed to learn a few things at the *Post*. For instance, I had navigated all over Long Island with a map (still astounding to me as, like many writers, I have a terrible sense of direction), plus I could now write headlines and captions, do an interview, compose drafts quickly, and type really fast—all skills that helped me in future jobs. It took me years to stop feeling stupid whenever I had to ask a question, but eventually I got over that, too.

Most of all, at the *Post*, I'd realized I didn't want to be a journalist. Not because of Carl or Jason or the long hours and poor pay. No, it was the stories themselves that made me see it. The information I cared about often ended up on the cutting-room floor. I had trouble writing news leads because I got caught up in the differences, for instance, in how subjects answered my questions, why one congresswoman called from her car and told me about her kids, while her male colleague read from a press release and spoke in a monotone. What did this tell me about them as people? As legislators? These kinds of details rarely fit into the "who, what, when, where, and why" of hard news. And even the human interest stories I wrote were never as compelling to me as the fictional ones I never stopped composing in my head.

When I walked out the door and down the steps for the last time, I swore I'd never again let someone else define the kind of writer I could or couldn't be, or demand that I tell certain parts of the story and not others. Lots of furious young journalists probably told themselves something similar as they walked away from that place. In my case, I can't say the *Post* was the last job I ever regretted, or that Carl was my last nasty boss, but as I got older, I found better jobs, allowing me more time to write fiction and tell the stories I wanted to tell.

SHARON POMERANTZ'S TIPS

▶ Do what you can to not feel so alone and powerless when you're in a terrible job; if you have to contract lice (or to even *pretend* that you've contracted lice) in order to get a day or two off to apply for other jobs, then do it.

▶ It's okay to trust your instinct that things are bad, and to look for a way out even when it seems too soon.

▶ Only you can determine your future; only you can decide who you will be.

PART IV

Learning Resilience

My graduate adviser, Stan Chu, wasn't smiling as we stood together outside of the third-grade classroom where he'd just watched me teach a reading lesson. This was the moment—at least in my mind—when he was supposed to "start with the positive," telling me about how great I was, followed by a couple of ways in which I might improve. Instead, he looked at me pointedly and said, "You must have asked those kids sixty different questions over the course of two minutes. There's no way *anyone*—let alone a child—can think when they're bombarded like that." I nodded, listening to him talk about the value of one *good* question, and felt my face get hot, my heart heavy. Here was a really nice guy, a professor whom I and all my grad school friends admired, who would probably say something positive about my teaching if there *was* anything positive to say. But I clearly sucked. At least that was how it felt.

* * *

It wasn't the first time that Stan was straight with me, and while this was sometimes hard on my ego, it helped me to see myself more clearly, as a teacher and as a person, and to understand mistakes as touchstones. They were learning opportunities if I could own them, take them apart, and think about how I might act differently next time. Eventually I learned that all thoughtful educators practice this process when they want to improve.

Learning from mistakes is not only integral to teaching; it's also an important part of doing scientific research. There is even a dedicated publication, *Journal of Errology*, which is *all about* screwing up. It publishes articles about failed experiments because, says the journal's website, "every discovery or invention has its fair share of missteps, failures, errors and problems, which result in teaching a valuable lesson and helping compound experience." What if more of us could see mistakes and failures as essential to doing our work well, to growing as people and professionals?

It's easier said than done. In a culture of achievement, our self-worth can become bound up in what and how much we accomplish. This is evident in the question that's often the first we ask in social situations: "What do you do?"—as if it will reveal who we are. It's also hard to see mistakes as learning opportunities because frankly, who wants to set a

goal and then fail to make it happen? Mistakes can be
embarrassing; they can feel *really bad*. But at the risk of
sounding a little like Mr. Rogers—it's okay to feel bad.
Even political candidate Reshma Saujani, something of an
Ivy League rock star, gave herself a full six weeks to mope
around with her puppy after losing an election. Then she
was back on the scene, as she discusses in the first section,
having learned important lessons. She was incredibly
resilient.

There are ways to increase your resilience—one of them,
probably the toughest to bear, is just surviving real-life
mistakes and failures. With mistakes at work, it also
helps to have the support of colleagues: Courtney Martin
talks here about a foot-in-mouth blogging error that
led to a major backlash; another blogger talked her
through it. Relationships with family and friends are
equally important: Judith Warner tells a story about
feeling depressed after losing a job, until finally one of her
daughters demanded she stop.

In the psychological literature on resilience, one of the
most well-respected ideas is Carol Dweck's theory of the
growth mindset versus the *fixed mindset*. Dweck, who
explains this in the last interview here, describes the ways
in which reframing our concept of ability can actually
help us to improve. "In the growth mindset," she says,

"you value learning and effort, and you see mistakes
and setbacks as tools for learning." It's not something that
you either have or don't have, though; you can work
toward developing a growth mindset in any area of your
life—at work, in your personal relationships, on the
athletic field.

I am putting my money on sharing stories as one more way
to bolster resilience, and others have, too. Harvard
University's Abigail Lipson runs something called the
Success-Failure Project, designed to create opportunities
for Harvard's high achievers to talk openly about what it's
like when things go wrong (as well as when things go
right—success has its own unique challenges). One of its
brilliant publications is a little red book called *Reflections
on Rejections*: it's full of rejection letters received by people
at Harvard, along with their own personal stories about
coping. Stanford University followed Lipson's model and
created something called the Resilience Project, a website
with videos of faculty, alumni, and students who talk
about (and thus model) dealing with difficult situations.
These projects open the door to important conversations,
and I hope that this book will do that as well. The brave,
amazing women who contributed are talking directly to
you, in some cases telling stories that they've never told
before, because they understand the importance of talking
about when things didn't go as planned. Even when that

felt absolutely terrible, they learned from what went wrong. Of course, you, too, can come to see mistakes as valuable information, contributing to your own metaphoric *Journal of Errology*, rich with the "data" of experiences that helped you to grow.

JUDITH WARNER

"Girls and young women are more susceptible to messages that they can be and do it all, that they can rise to levels of impossible perfection and performance. When I see statistics showing that girls are outperforming boys, I think it's a girl crisis and not—as some have written—a 'boy crisis.'"

I crossed my fingers that Judith Warner would agree to an interview because I love her writing. Printed copies of her articles are always scattered across my desk because she writes so eloquently about the pressures young women face. For example, in her response to a widely circulated piece about high-achieving girls, Warner wrote in the *New York Times*: "Many, I think, never figure out how to handle the emptiness that comes when the rush of achievement fades away, or the loneliness—the sense of invisibility—when no one is there to hand out yet another 'A.' The fact is: when you are narrowly programmed to achieve, you are like a windup toy with only one movement in its repertoire." During our conversation, I mentioned this article to Warner. She told me that when she wrote it, back in 2007, she hadn't quite figured out her *own* relationship to achievement. However, it may be *because* she was able to relate to the high achievers that she was able to write so incisively about the pressures that young people face.

Warner is best known for her 2005 *New York Times* best-seller, *Perfect Madness: Motherhood in the Age of Anxiety*, and for her beloved *New York Times* column, Domestic Disturbances. Her latest book, *We've Got Issues: Children and Parents in the Age of Medication*, received multiple awards, including a 2010 Outstanding Media Award for Science and Health Reporting from the National Alliance on Mental Illness. Warner is currently a contributing writer for the *New York Times Magazine* and an opinion columnist for Time.com, as well as a senior fellow at the Center for American Progress and a 2012–13 recipient of a Rosalynn Carter Fellowship for Mental Health Journalism. She lives in Washington, DC.

Lessons I've Learned

Don't let a difficult work situation keep you from trying to get the most that you can out of the experience.

I made the same mistake in my very first job out of college and in another job, twenty-two years later: doubting myself. My first job was in 1987 at a prestigious training program that the *New York Times* used to have, called the Writing Program. The Writing Program hired its participants to do clerical work but offered the opportunity to report and write as many stories as you could in your spare time. After about eighteen months you would be evaluated, and if they liked your stories then you would get a brief reporting stint. If you did really well with *that*, then you would get hired as a reporter, which of course was the ultimate goal.

I loved the *New York Times* and was thrilled to get the job. But my excitement waned when the woman who ran the program told me, "You're being hired with one big caveat: you are a much weaker candidate than all the others, and the editors feel you're going to have to work twice as hard as everyone else in order to succeed." Now, she probably meant, "You've done a lot of features and opinion writing but not much hard news, and we feel you should focus on getting hard news experience." But I interpreted it as an insult rather than a challenge, and as a result, I came in and felt as if they didn't really want or like me.

It was a combination of this introduction to the job and my own lack of commitment about what I wanted to be—I thought I might go into academia or become a fiction writer—that led to not making the most of my time there. For example, there was a chance to be a temporary clerk at the Boston bureau, and I said no because I wanted to take a screenwriting class. In retrospect, if you are lucky enough to be in a place like the *New York Times*, you don't say no to opportunities that come along. You recognize that you are lucky to have them. And I didn't somehow, because I was so busy living my own inner drama. The initial comments made by the woman who ran the program certainly didn't help to motivate me; they just made me feel bad about myself. Looking back, having a different attitude and making the most of it would have been a more resilient approach. It would take me a long time, however, to realize that my feelings about the experience were a result of my own fear.

When a blow comes your way, you don't have to lie down and die.

After leaving the *Times*, I began freelancing. At first I wasn't getting a lot of work, but things started taking off in the early nineties. I married and had children, and I wrote one of my most successful books, *Perfect Madness*, after coming back to the United States with my family from Paris and comparing the social supports for families available in France to the anxious free-for-all that was American motherhood. In 2006, eighteen years and a number of books after my initial *New York Times* stint, I was offered an opportunity to write an online column called Domestic Disturbances. It had started as a blog about my everyday life, but the editor, Gail Collins, wanted to turn it into something permanent. This was beyond a dream come true: I was part of the *New York Times*, I had my own column, and the subject, which widened to be about what we called "the politics of everyday life," was endlessly fascinating to me. I loved working for Collins and enjoyed the back-and-forth with *New York Times* readers—I learned a lot from their comments and critiques.

I wrote Domestic Disturbances for nearly four years. At the same time I was developing my latest book, *We've Got Issues*, and was working hard with minimal child care because I wanted to be around for my daughters after school. The effects of my workload started wearing on me. I was having chronic migraines; I was not getting out and seeing people; I was stressed but was not admitting it to myself or anyone else. When you're caught up in external signs of success, you don't necessarily take care of yourself in ways that lead to personal sustainability. This undermines resilience because at a certain point you crash and burn.

In the winter of 2009, I learned that the *New York Times* wasn't renewing my contract. I was devastated. It was a huge blow to my confidence. I'm not somebody who normally suffers from depression, but it was like going down into a black hole. Granted, some of that "get up and fight" instinct is hardwired and temperamental and some people are naturally more resilient than others. But I think problems arise in particular for someone like me: because school had always come easily, the first twenty-two years of my life had been a string of successes, and I didn't really know how to handle setbacks.

When I lost the column, my daughters were just entering the teen years. At the time, I was reading a book by the psychologist Madeline Levine, and it began with an anecdote about a girl who spent her whole life striving to get into a specific college. When she didn't get in, she was laid out flat in bed with depression. It struck so close to home, and I thought,

"This is a real cautionary tale, this valuing yourself through externals."

I went through a process of grieving and then it started to lift. I was sick of listening to the negativity running through my head, sick of dressing in yoga pants all the time. And part of what got me off my ass was my daughter saying, "Enough already. This is getting ridiculous." I began talking to people; reconnecting to relationships that were important to me helped to pull me out of myself.

Be open to external validation that comes from sources other than your usual ones.

My most recent book, *We've Got Issues*, which challenges commonly held beliefs about families struggling with their children's mental health issues, came out in February 2010, which was around the time when my *Times* contract ended. It didn't sell as well as my previous book had, and I remember the publisher awkwardly and reluctantly calling me to share the low sales figures while I was on my book tour. Initially, this compounded my feelings of failure.

But here's the amazing thing: in the long term, writing that book has been the most enriching, validating professional experience I've ever had. I was invited to speak all over the country because parents, educators, doctors, and mental health professionals loved it. The book won three awards—I'd never won awards before! Subsequently, I've kept expanding my knowledge of the area. I received a fellowship from the Carter Center to take the research further and write a book proposal on the history of the idea of the "difficult child" and of child psychiatry in America. As a result of these experiences, I've become less concerned with "building my name" as a journalist and more concerned with doing work that actually helps people and makes a difference in their lives—either by bringing information that's helpful to them or by making them feel less alone.

At the same time, I can't say, "I learned from my experience and changed," because that wouldn't be entirely honest. I'm still the same person: driven, hopeful for external validation, and sometimes hard on myself. But I've learned compensatory strategies to balance myself out—like getting out of the house long enough to forget about that voice of self-criticism. I'm also more compassionate toward myself and others.

Back in the first job at the *Times*, it would have been great if I could have said, "Even though the head of the clerical workers is telling me I'm 'less than,' this is an amazing opportunity and I'm going to see every day as a learning experience." I've only come to have that kind of attitude in the past couple of years. If you can start to develop it early, it's a great attitude for getting through life.

JUDITH WARNER'S TIPS

Note from Judith: I don't think of myself as someone who gives tips, but I am throwing these out there anyway.

▶ Always remember to think about all the potential for learning in any environment. Even if that means nothing more than viewing it anthropologically, because first jobs are often not very good, there may be something fascinating about the people or the way things are done.

▶ If you're not blessed enough to be able to banish the voice of self-doubt and self-criticism from your head, then develop compensatory strategies—like getting out of the house, exercising, and connecting with friends.

RINKU SEN

"Sometimes you are able to see things that people around you are not able to see, either because of the way your mind works or because of your personal interests or because of the things you're exposed to. When you have an innovative idea that your colleagues may not quite be ready to embrace, there's a balance between not getting too far ahead of them (so that you have no help) and pandering to their resistance, which could have many sources."

"Everyone thought I was crazy," says Rinku Sen when she talks about initiating a campaign called "Drop the I-Word," aimed at erasing the words "illegal" and "illegals" from the public discourse on immigrants. But it was the influence of this campaign and of Sen's organization, the Applied Research Center (ARC), that caused the Associated Press (AP) to announce in 2013 that it would no longer use the dehumanizing term "illegal" to describe people who were immigrants in the United States. Because news sources nationwide are guided by "AP Style," this was a major victory—and just one example of the ways in which Sen has been an innovative leader and risk taker in advocating for racial justice.

Rinku Sen began her organizing career as a student activist

in college; since then, she has combined journalism and activism to make social change. As ARC's president and the publisher of its news website, Colorlines.com, she has positioned the organization as a national home for media, research, and activism on issues related to racial justice. She is the recipient of numerous fellowships and awards for activists and journalists, including being named a Prime Movers fellow and one of *Ms.* magazine's "21 Feminists to Watch." Her work on immigration has recently been featured on ABC and MSNBC.

Sen received a BA in women's studies at Brown University in 1988 and an MS in journalism at Columbia University in 2005. A native of India, she grew up in the northeastern factory towns and learned to speak English in a two-room schoolhouse.

Lessons I've Learned

Resistance from colleagues is not the same as "no."

My family came to the United States from India in 1972, when I was five and a half years old. I took my cues about how to be an American from Marcia Brady, down to wanting to eat hot dogs and pizza for dinner because that's what I thought Americans did. I developed a kind of allergy to thinking of myself as a person of color because we always lived in small, very white towns. My friends thought of themselves as Americans and my parents thought of themselves as Indians. There wasn't a slot for me.

But things changed when I went to college. During my second year, a black freshman was beaten up by two white football players, and the incident sparked an on-campus campaign for racial justice. My friends wanted me to join them at a rally and I told them, "No, that's not for me. That's not who I am."

"Listen, Rinku," they said, "you're a person of color and you're a woman—it's time to grow up and get involved."

I went to the rally and it changed my life. For the first time since I'd arrived in the United States, I felt like I actually belonged somewhere. I understood that being an American was not about being just like the families I saw on TV or eating particular foods: it was about working to make your community more inclusive, more compassionate, and more effective.

I became a campus organizer, and after graduation I became a community organizer. Years later, journalism school led to a position as director of the Applied Research Center, crafting a media-driven strategy for the racial justice movement and being the publisher of its print magazine, *Colorlines*.

Colorlines had a subscriber base of around twelve hundred when in 2003, I proposed that we needed what was then called a "weblog." We'd be able to include many more writers, to be more timely, and to potentially reach more people. But the feedback from my staff meeting was negative and strong.

Who would read it?

How would we let the world know about it?

What did it have to do with our core mission and day-to-day work?

Of course, I had no answers to those questions, and I felt that there was no point in developing answers unless we were actually going to pursue the idea. I told my colleagues that we could figure all that out, but they didn't have any examples and couldn't imagine a "weblog" as a part of their work lives. Instead of doing some research so that I'd be able to answer their questions, I gave up, feeling defensive and dismissed, wondering why they couldn't "get with the program."

We didn't talk about it again for another three years. In 2007 we finally started a blog, which immediately got four thousand hits a week. When it became clear that we'd reach many more people by taking the entire magazine online, we did so in 2010. We went from having twelve hundred print subscribers to reaching tens of thousands of people within the first month of launching. It was very clear that the Internet was the right way to go. But how much ahead of the game would we have been by starting years earlier?

The lesson is: resistance is just resistance. If you make a conscious decision not to pursue your idea, that's one thing. But unless somebody says, "No, don't do that," it's *not* a no. And if you allow yourself to be dissuaded without actually hearing that no, then you may end up feeling like a victim and feeling resentful at work.

Having said that, I've since come to understand—through experience and observation—that questions are not always questions. Sometimes people are advocating for their own opinions. For example, someone might ask something like, "How does this relate to the work we do now?" and they are really saying, "This *doesn't* relate to the work we do now, but I don't want to *say* that, because it's Rinku and I don't want to hurt her feelings." When colleagues are unable to be respectfully forthright, communication at work becomes a lot less productive.

Happily, I had good relationships with my colleagues and we were able to move forward. But it's important to understand that women in particular are raised not to disagree, especially with people whom they respect and like and want to support, or when there is some power inequality. It can feel safer to ask a question than to make an assertion. As a leader, you need to make people comfortable enough to undo that habit. I've learned to sometimes balance my direct leadership style with probing questions so that colleagues feel encouraged to say what they want to say.

Doing good work requires learning to deal with defensive feelings.

When I first started working, I did not receive negative feedback well. My immediate reaction was always to act defensively. I distinctly recall one of the first times I received criticism on the job. I was twenty-three years old and had taken over the Center for Third World Organizing with a codirector. We hired a twenty-one-year-old South Asian woman as an intern, and at the end of the internship, she told me that I had disappointed her. Among her criticisms, she said that I hadn't met her expectations as a South Asian woman mentor. This made me feel terrible and, looking back, I know that I didn't react well.

Instead of asking, "What do you think I could have done better? What might you have expected?" I said something dismissive that shut her down on the spot. I remember thinking, "That can't be true. I did everything I could. It's *her* fault." I had supervised her, assigned projects to her, and checked their quality. But looking back, I know now that she wanted a more personal relationship and I just wasn't ready for that.

I've since learned that taking a "screw that" attitude doesn't allow for growth. These days, if a criticism upsets me, I'll ask for a break. For example, I might say, "I'm really feeling what you've just put in front of me, and I would like to take a minute to process it. Could we talk again in a half hour?" (Or tomorrow—depending on how much time I'd like.) We often think everything has to happen *right now*, especially when we're unsettled emotionally, but it doesn't.

Over the years, I became increasingly self-aware, able to step back and see when a comment or situation was making me feel defensive—but even now, it can still be tough to receive negative feedback. For example, last year I led a racial justice training for a group of people in a format that I'd used many times and trusted was effective. Ninety percent of the time, participants respond to this workshop afterward by saying things like, "You've changed my life," and "This is the best training I've ever attended." But with this particular training, people said things that no one *ever* says about me: that I was insensitive, that I seemed distracted and snappy. One person even said, "She can't facilitate large groups."

I immediately wanted to do things to fix the situation: I imagined writing a long e-mail explaining myself or asking a colleague to talk to the client on my behalf.

Instead, I called a close colleague who knows me well and could offer support and perspective. We talked for about twenty minutes and she asked instructive questions: What was I most concerned about in the feedback? How might I get more information about what might have happened? She reminded me that people have off days, and that I shouldn't stew over it, and I knew she was right. Having her perspective was helpful—I managed not to get all churned up about the incident and instead thought of a balanced, productive plan.

First, I scheduled a debriefing call with the client, and as we discussed the workshop I'd led, I realized that I *had* been somewhat distracted. I came to understand—all over again—that because talking about race and racial justice is so charged, I have to be fully present when I lead such a discussion. I decided that in the future, if I felt distracted or overwhelmed going into a workshop, I would ask for help. And I decided to write a brief note to the group I'd led, thanking them for their feedback and saying that I had taken it seriously.

Having the discipline to not be defensive shouldn't be confused with unnecessarily taking responsibility—but the reason you don't want to react in the moment is so that you can gather more information about the situation and determine "What's mine to take? What's really not?" You can respond to the criticism later, saying, "I've thought hard about what you raised. These are the things I acknowledge and would change. But I want to raise the possibility that there might be some shared responsibility here." Give yourself enough time to gain clarity. In any work situation, slowing down and being reflective before a tough conversation can make all the difference.

RINKU SEN'S TIPS

▶ Develop a habit of listening to other people and taking their concerns and questions seriously without overinternalizing their resistance to your ideas.

▶ When someone is criticizing you, don't "check out" or dwell on defensive thoughts, like, "She can keep talking, but it's not affecting me." Keep your reaction minimal, and ask for more details. Do some soul-searching to figure out "What is this person saying that I really need to own and change?"

▶ We don't control everything, and sometimes we make mistakes, and not everybody loves us. It's part of taking risks and doing the work.

SHIRLEY MALCOM

"When I was a kid, I went to kindergarten, skipped first grade, and started school in the second grade. For many years afterward, I had a recurring dream that people found this out and were going to make me go back to first grade and pass it, and the biggest problem was that I didn't fit in the chairs anymore. I didn't stop having the dream until I had finished my PhD, because I think I somehow knew that I hadn't gotten where I was going yet."

Dr. Shirley Malcom believes that science is often taught the wrong way: through rote memorization of terminology and with "recipes" for experiments that tell kids to follow certain steps, explaining what the results of those steps will be. Instead, Dr. Malcom says, children should have the opportunity to learn scientific concepts through coming up with their own questions, then conducting real research to try to find the answers. "I'm not saying there's not drudgery in science," she told a *New York Times* reporter, "but when you get to the point where all the data are sitting in front of you and you start seeing patterns and nature begins to speak—that's a kick."

Dr. Malcom has dedicated much of her life to making sure that all kinds of people have access to quality education in the STEM fields (science, technology, engineering, and math). As director of the Education and Human Resources Programs of the American Association for the Advancement of Science, she leads a division that develops programs in education and activities for underrepresented groups and works toward increased public understanding of science and technology.

During the Clinton administration, Dr. Malcom served on the National Science Board and on the President's Council of Advisors on Science and Technology. She has sat on and chaired several other boards as well and has worked as a trustee for institutions like the Carnegie Corporation and the American Museum of Natural History. In 2003 Dr. Malcom received the Public Welfare Medal of the National Academy of Sciences, the highest award given by the academy.

Dr. Malcom earned a PhD in ecology from Pennsylvania State University and a master's in zoology from UCLA. She graduated with distinction and a BA in zoology from the University of Washington. She also holds sixteen honorary degrees.

Lessons I've Learned

Having a limited understanding of what you can do with your college major can confine you to a career path that may not be right for you.

Growing up black in Birmingham, Alabama, in the 1950s, I had a lot of practice being told that I couldn't do things. Our church was bombed multiple times because it was led by a minister who was active in the civil rights movement. Our governor, George Wallace, was sending out the message that the state wouldn't invest in black kids because they weren't as good as white kids and wouldn't amount to anything. In that type of divisive environment, you can either buy into it or you can basically say, "Up yours." So my response was to prove them wrong. I was an "up yours" kind of girl.

I was good at science and math and graduated from high school at sixteen with all A's. My parents wanted me to be challenged in college, but we weren't sure where I should go because southern universities were essentially segregated. You could attend a historically black college with limited resources because the state government was starving those institutions, or you could be one of the first students to "integrate" an all-white college. The idea of being thrust in as one of the first few black students in a vitriolic, segregationist culture wasn't appealing, and so I made the decision to move away from home and attend the University of Washington in Seattle. My aunt, uncle, and older sister lived in Seattle, so we knew I'd have family close by, and we also knew that it was an especially tolerant city.

Living on the university campus was a total shock. I had grown up in an all-black environment where the people in my neighborhood looked like me, my teachers looked like me. Now all of a sudden, I was having a hard time finding even a *handful* of African Americans. After the end of the first year, I was the only African American student in an eight-hundred-person dorm; in my big introductory science classes, I was one

of two or three African Americans. It was discomforting, not
because I needed to be around others who looked like me in
order to learn but because I was young to be suddenly surrounded by a world that was so different from the one in which
I'd grown up.

Some of what I saw and heard was confusing. For example, all my female friends who were African American expected that after college they would work—and that they'd
always have to work. But white friends seemed to think their
careers should be subservient to those of their spouses—many
thought they'd eventually be housewives despite their educational backgrounds. One of my friends abandoned her pre-
med program to pursue a teaching credential so she'd be able
to support her fiancé in medical school. Then, in senior year,
he dumped her. I tried to be supportive, but I didn't understand why anyone would thwart her own ambitions in order to
accommodate those of her fiancé, and I thought: *She doesn't get
it.* I had been raised with this notion that knowledge is something nobody can take away from you. It's great that she became a teacher; but I was never comfortable that this was her
choice. I began to understand that many black women's views
about education were different from what I was seeing out of
my white sisters.

Throughout college, I maintained above a B average and
planned to be a doctor, but at that time medical schools had
quotas, and an incoming class was unlikely to be more than 10
percent female. I'll never forget the day I met with my pre-med

adviser and she looked at my 3.0 GPA from the first semester—freshman year!—then told me I should probably forget about medical school altogether. I'd need *better* grades than the guys in order to be admitted among that 10 percent. I said okay and then ignored her; if I'd taken what she said as gospel, I would have shut down because it would have meant I couldn't pursue my dream. I understood that she wasn't trying to be mean, just honest, but it was a bit of a shock because, quite frankly, as an African American woman I hadn't been told that "women don't do" this, that, or the other. Now all of a sudden the limiting factor wasn't just about being African American—it was also about being female.

A lot of women at the University of Washington were premed, and I watched as many dropped out—probably discouraged by conversations like the one my adviser had had with me—and others stayed in but didn't bother applying to medical school because they knew they'd be discriminated against. I persevered and took the MCATs during the spring semester of my junior year but began to realize that I really didn't like the other pre-meds. They were mostly men, and they were pretty terrible. I remember one time when I was carrying a giant dead cat from the animal room into the lab for dissection, and a group of male students went ahead of me and then let the door slam back in my face. Another time, a male student actually said to me, "Why do you want to go to medical school? Don't you realize that you're taking some guy's place?" And I said something like, "Well, it's only his place if he earns it." But I just couldn't imagine the idea of four more years with these obnoxious people who felt so entitled, and I began to think that maybe I was only a pre-med because I didn't know what else you could do with science.

My major was actually zoology, and when my adviser asked, "Well, why not academic science? Why not go for the PhD?" I decided to hit the reset button. I thought this guy hung the moon, and I figured that if he thought I could do it, then maybe I should try.

*If you take a break from schooling and plan to return,
do it before you get bogged down with other demands.*

Instead of going to medical school, I entered a doctoral program in zoology at UCLA. The year was 1967 and the world was just starting to go nuts. The Vietnam War was raging, the women's movement was taking off, and all of a sudden it was like everything was changing or being questioned. Young people were challenging the beliefs and behavior of their elders, whether about civil rights or women's rights or Chicano or Latino rights or about the war. And the leaders who were drawing attention to these injustices were falling one by one: Dr. King, Robert Kennedy, and Malcom X were all assassinated within months of each other. You just stopped and wondered, Who's next?

There were a lot of earthquakes during that time, real,

physical earthquakes. One leveled a wing of the veterans' hospital in the valley in 1971 and had hundreds of aftershocks. These earthquakes almost manifested as a physical representation of my generation's emotional turmoil. We wanted to create cultural change and were rejecting a lot of what had always been in place. On the day that UCLA students took over the administration building and shut down the entire institution, I began to wonder: "What am I doing here? What does studying zoology have to do with what's going on in the world? How does my life as a graduate student relate to the struggles that are under way everywhere?" And so I decided to take a leave of absence to regroup—it seemed the smartest thing to do at the time—and to teach high school in Los Angeles.

While I was teaching, I became close with my cousin and his wife who lived in L.A. They had a little girl, and during the time we were friends, she became pregnant again and had a baby boy. She was getting ready to go back to school and start a doctoral program in education when I heard the horrible news that she had been murdered. It was the kind of terrible story that you never imagine will touch anyone close to you: the murderer was actually a woman with whom my friend's husband—my cousin—had briefly had an affair. On the day that my friend was killed, I was the person who went over to the house to help care for my friend's two-and-a-half-year-old and her three-month-old baby. I was making baby formula and comforting the kids and the aunt and the relatives back in Birmingham; I was talking with the police; I was shoring up my cousin, who was nearly suicidal with guilt. At only twenty-four years old, I was trying to be the strong one in the midst of a nightmare, but that can take a toll.

After a couple of weeks, the children were sent to stay with their grandparents in Birmingham, and I knew I couldn't stay in California, either—I was completely devastated and also exhausted because dealing with that kind of trauma just tears you apart. I gave up my teaching job and left Los Angeles to go home to my parents' house. All I wanted to do was hide my head under a pillow.

During the following year, I realized that I had to figure out who I was and where I was going. I started to realize that there's a time to get yourself together, but at a certain point you may be as together as you're likely to get. Because of the death of my friend, I came to understand that life is short, and I would have to find my way through this. I didn't want to put off doing things that were important to me, because I understood that nothing was guaranteed. I began looking around for employment opportunities someplace else. A friend who knew about the incident told me about a job opening in Seattle, so I went there for a bit and then started applying to graduate school again.

I was accepted into a doctor of arts in teaching program at Penn State. Upon my arrival, I went to a professor to get approval for his seminar in animal behavior. He looked at the transcript of what I'd done in my doctoral program and said, "The last thing you need is more coursework. You need to just do your doctoral research and get out of here." He asked me to leave the teaching program and come and do a PhD in ecology as his advisee, and that's what I did. Almost two years to the day after I entered his program, I defended my dissertation.

When you are one of the only people from a particular cultural background—in a classroom, a workplace, or an entire field—any bias that you face is complicated by being female.

After graduate school, I had a faculty position at the University of North Carolina at Wilmington, but I left in 1975 when I married, as my husband was in the DC area. I didn't have a job when I moved there, but found a position in the want ads as a research assistant at the American Association for the Advancement of Science. We were working on a project to identify initiatives that were increasing the participation of minorities in the STEM fields. I felt so gratified to be doing this kind of work that I would have done it for free if I could have afforded it, because throughout college, graduate school, and the early years of my career, I had always wondered where everybody else was— *why* there were so few women of color studying and working around me. I began talking to people who were interested in this issue. My boss and mentor applied for a National Science Foundation grant to lead a study and hold a conference on minority women in the sciences.

Women who came to the conference talked about trying to get their research and work done while managing—both logistically and emotionally—the things that happened to them because they were black women or Latina women or Native American women. Early on, racism had affected their school experiences; for example, they might have had advisers who didn't know how to relate to them because of their different backgrounds. But as their careers progressed, they'd become increasingly aware of predefined expectations about how high women could rise or what they could achieve. One biology professor talked about being asked to turn over her lab space to a male scientist with an "of course you'll understand" attitude. We coined a term, "the double bind," for the phenomenon of being caught between racism and sexism, and that term is still in use today.

I had my own stories to bring to the table. One prime example was an experience that I'd had when I filled an unexpired vacancy on the National Science Board. There were twenty-five people on the board; I was the second woman in that particular group and the only African American. I had previously been a program officer for the National Science Foundation and was fluent in the language of public policy; however, some assumed that I was an affirmative action appointment to the National Science Board. When I came to those meetings and had something to offer beyond the topic of diversity, people seemed genuinely surprised. And when I did my homework and challenged them because what they were saying didn't make sense in light of what they should have read, I could tell that some of my colleagues hadn't anticipated that.

What became clear at that seminal convergence of female scientists of color—and in the subsequent paper that we wrote detailing our findings—was that the costs of becoming a scientist are high, but that when you add any level of difference, the costs are higher. As more women and more women of color enter the sciences, hopefully this will change. My current role at the American Association for the Advancement of Science means that I'm in charge of a wide-ranging strategy to reach underrepresented groups and make programs in science and technology education available to everyone.

Many years after the bombing of my grandmother's church, when I was a grown-up, I saw the movie Spike Lee made about it, *4 Little Girls*, and was amazed by a quick archival video clip of our church's minister hugging my grandmother on the day after the bombing. I had been ten at the time but still remembered everything so vividly: my grandmother wanted me to walk down to the church with her; the moment when she saw her pastor she ran up and hugged him. I had stood there, watching the people who were around. The church was a shambles and the parsonage was gone. Just obliterated.

When I went online many years later to find that clip, I saw something else just off to the right: a little girl. I had no idea that *I* had been captured in the footage. It made me think about how the ten-year-old me would have been really surprised at where the sixty-six-year-old me is now. She would never have imagined the things that I've had an opportunity to do, the people I've had an opportunity to know. She would never have imagined the things that I've had to overcome and the things that have come my way. And it made me think that you never know, when you see a kid, where the pathway of that kid is going to lead. You have to look at her as representing a future and a talent that we can only imagine, if she's given the opportunity.

SHIRLEY MALCOM'S TIPS

▶ The respect of colleagues can bring its own set of issues. For example, people may describe you with an attached modifier: you're a *qualified* minority or an *articulate* minority. They use adjectives to cut you out of the herd. Early in my career, I ignored this and kept doing the good work that I was doing; as I got older, I sometimes took them on, asking, "What do you mean?" I think that you have to respond in the way that feels right to you.

▶ Even when we have to step back or step out of college or graduate school, it's important to get back into the mix before you lose a sense of how to study, before your knowledge becomes old, before you acquire debt or a family or a lot of other things that may keep you from moving ahead.

RUTH OZEKI

"A mistake is a retrospective judgment—we don't deem something a 'mistake' until time has passed. It really has a lot to do with how critical you are of your past, how you judge it, and the kind of philosophy you have about the way life unfolds or emerges."

Ruth Ozeki's latest book, *A Tale for the Time Being*, takes place—in part—in Japan. She had nearly completed it in 2011 and was about to give it to her editor when events in Japan made her realize that she'd need to rework the entire narrative. As she told interviewer Rachel Martin on NPR, "The earthquake in Japan happened, followed by the tsunami and the meltdown at Fukushima. And suddenly, as I was watching all of this unfold, I realized that Japan would never be the same and that the book that I had written was no longer relevant." She changed the novel in a way that would allow her to explore and respond to those events, and it was published to sparkling reviews—the *Washington Post* called it "as emotionally engaging as it is intellectually provocative." It was shortlisted for the prestigious Man Booker Prize.

Ozeki, a graduate of Smith College, has worked in television and has made several independent films, including 1995's

Halving the Bones, which tells the story of her journey during the process of bringing her grandmother's remains home from Japan. It has been screened at the Sundance Film Festival, the Museum of Modern Art, the Montreal World Film Festival, and the Margaret Mead Film Festival, among others. She came to writing after productive careers in both industries and published her first novels, *My Year of Meats* and *All Over Creation*, to critical acclaim when she was in her forties. During that time, Ozeki also began studying to become a Zen Buddhist priest. When the Man Booker Prize committee announced its nominations online, it said: "This is surely . . . the first time a filmmaking Zen-Buddhist priest . . . has been included on the longlist."

Lessons I've Learned

Remorse can be artistically motivating.

My father was a wonderful man but he was a terrible perfectionist and, like many perfectionists, he procrastinated. At the end of his life, he was tormented by remorse about all the things he hadn't gotten around to doing. I think the root cause of procrastination is probably fear—fear of making mistakes, but also fear of losing control. Dying is all about losing control, and as I watched my father suffer, I made a vow to do everything I could not to wind up plagued by remorse like his. I could see myself in him. I had inherited his perfectionist streak and his controlling tendencies. And I procrastinated.

If procrastination is a symptom of perfectionism, it's also a protective strategy—you stop yourself before you can make a mistake. It's not an effective strategy, but it's a strategy none-theless. At Smith College, whenever I had papers to write or a test to study for, I used to procrastinate, and it became a habit. It's a terrible feeling. You know that you need to do something, but you engage in all kinds of denial in order to avoid it. I managed to get through my four years, but I caused myself an enormous amount of grief and suffering.

At the time when my father was dying and I was witness-ing his proclamations of regret, I was forty-one years old and finishing my first novel. Being with him caused me to reflect back on my own life and behavior, and it occurred to me then that maybe writing fiction was my way of coming to terms with my regrets. Maybe it was also a way of cultivating a kinder, more generous, and even appreciative attitude toward my own mistakes.

If you are a fiction writer, or I suppose any kind of writer, you learn to value your mistakes because they have the potential to generate material. Someone once said that writers write out of remorse, and I think that's somewhat true. The remorse that you feel over mistakes you've made in the past is like the irritant, the grain of sand in the oyster shell, around which a new work ag-gregates. Now, as I look back at the novels that I've written, each one of them has been inspired by some irritant, some mistake, some misstep or misjudgment that I made and then couldn't forget. The novel then becomes a formal way of exploring it.

The inspiration for my first book, for example, came from the work I did in the television business during the 1980s. I used to work for Japanese TV, and during that period I was asked to do a variety of different things, which I might not have gone along with had I stopped to examine them. I don't know if I would call these mistakes, exactly, but they did cause me some ethical misgivings.

One example was a documentary series we made called *New Yorker*, about cool hip New Yorkers' lifestyles. The show was sponsored by the Philip Morris tobacco company, and in each episode, we were required to include a shot of a preferably beautiful and young New Yorker smoking a Philip Morris cigarette—it was kind of a subliminal, sneaky ad within the body of what purported to be a documentary. This was at a time when Americans were growing more health conscious and cigarette smoking was losing popularity in the United States, and so the big tobacco companies were redirecting their TV advertising budgets to expand their Asian markets. I had been a smoker for years myself, and I was trying very hard to quit, but there I'd be with my crew, handing out Marlboros and matches to young beautiful people on the street, asking if we could film them smoking. It was awkward and embarrassing, and we didn't like it, but we did it anyway, and because I was addicted to cigarettes myself, I felt like a total hypocrite.

Around that same time, I was working on a proposal for a documentary series called *Mrs. America*, profiling the lives of interesting and diverse American women. Again this was in the 1980s, and women in Japan didn't have the kinds of opportunities that American women had, a situation which I and many of my female colleagues found disturbing. We had a subversive feminist agenda to use mainstream network television to bring images of strong, powerful American women leading interesting lives to housewives in Japan—at least this was our intention.

We were always pitching new ideas for shows to the head office in Tokyo, but only a few of these ever made it past the drawing board stage—that's just the nature of the business. So when I learned that the series had been picked up for sponsorship, I was thrilled because it meant the show would actually go into production. Even when I learned that the sponsor was the U.S. Meat Export Federation and that they wanted us to turn it into a cooking show, I didn't really balk. We just went ahead and produced the show, featuring stories of interesting American women, their lifestyles, their families—and their delicious recipes for beef.

I didn't think much about what it meant to be sponsored by a meat industry lobby group. None of us did. We were happy to have steady work. We were happy to launch our feminist Trojan horse. I knew that there was something unsavory about the meat industry, but I also knew I couldn't "go there."

Most of what I knew about the industry at the time was, and is, common knowledge. Meat animals are raised on large factory farms, where they're often treated inhumanely. The effluent from feedlots pollutes rivers and watersheds. South American rain forests are being cut down to create grazing land for cattle. But for me, at the time when I was producing the show, this was all passive knowledge. I *kind of* knew it, but it was inconvenient to think about, and so I didn't.

Still, there was something—some irritant or kernel of remorse—that continued to niggle and worry me, and years later, when I left the TV industry and became a writer, I returned to this episode in my life and made it the subject of my first novel, *My Year of Meats*. The novel tells the story of two women, on opposite sides of the planet, connected by a TV cooking show: one woman is a documentary filmmaker in New York who is hired to make the show, sponsored by the meat industry; the other is a Tokyo housewife who watches the show and cooks the featured meats.

In the novel, the New York filmmaker (and my alter ego), Jane Takagi-Little, talks about passive knowledge and ignorance—how ignorance derives from what we choose to ignore. "In this root sense," she says, "ignorance is an act of will, a choice that one makes over and over again." My ignorance, my decision to ignore what I kind of knew, became the subject of the novel, and I finally took the time to research commercial meat production and learn about the industry that I'd been promoting for all those years. Of course, I was shocked.

Everything I'd kind of known turned out to be true, only it was worse than I'd expected. I discovered disturbing information about the industrywide practice of administering large doses of pharmaceuticals—growth hormones and antibiotics—to cattle. I learned that the European Union had banned American meat in Europe because of the use of growth hormones, to which the U.S. meat producers responded by using their Washington trade lobbyists to pressure Japan into signing a new beef agreement, increasing the amount of American red meat imported to Japan. And I realized how and where my little story had fit into this historical moment: my program, *Mrs. America*, was launched shortly after the new beef agreement was signed.

Reflecting on moments when you wish you'd behaved differently can help you to develop as an ethical person.

In retrospect, I understand why I did what I did. I needed to pay the rent, and it was all happening so fast, and anyway working in TV is fun! It makes you feel powerful, important, and special—sublimely entitled. (If you've ever seen a television crew or a film crew at work, you can feel the entitlement emanating from them.) There's a lot of money involved and a lot of pressure to get things done quickly. Every minute of production time costs hundreds, even thousands of dollars, and

as a worker in the industry, you're not really encouraged
to spend this valuable time attending to your ethical qualms
and scruples or parsing the questions of conscience that might
arise. If you're going to be in that world, you just go along
with it.

For a fiction writer, however, minutes are cheap, and no
one cares how you while away your days, so I was able to spend
long hours sitting with my niggling remorse, studying it and
trying to put words to it. *My Year of Meats* grew out of my reflections on the kinds of ethical dilemmas I'd faced, or failed
to face, while earning a living in commercial television. It grew
out of my discomfort with the decisions that I had made, producing documentaries that purported to tell the truth but
which were, in fact, highly constructed corporate-sponsored
semifictions. In order to write the book, I had to reenter that
mindset and that body and almost live it again. I was able to
mull over my questions and understand where my choices had
come from.

I also came to understand more about the workings of ignorance. We often blame our ignorance for our mistakes, but if
you think of ignorance not as a passive condition but rather as
an active choice, then it is actually quite empowering. Ignorance is an act of will, and so is knowledge. We can just as easily choose not to be ignorant. We can choose not to ignore the
conditions of the world. We can take responsibility for our mistakes, rather than avoiding them, engage with our remorse,
and stop living in fear and denial.

The process of writing fiction is a process of reflection, but it's more than that, because it's creative and generative as well. You look back on the past, but you also construct and test alternate realities. You consider the what-ifs. What if I had taken the time to really understand these things back then? What if I had acted differently? It's a bit of an exercise in wishful thinking, and it's nourished by mistakes and the remorse you feel for making them. Chances are that every time you act, every time you do anything in the world, you won't get it perfectly right. So you always have something to chew on, and this is not a bad thing.

The wonderful thirteenth-century Zen master Dogen Zenji used a phrase to describe being alive that translates as "one continuous mistake." It just means that life is a long series of mistakes, each of which generates a new set of causes and conditions, which then lead you to your next mistake. Each mistake is an opportunity to step back and examine your behavior, your thoughts, and your words, and to reevaluate and make some kind of adjustment. And so every mistake is an opportunity to learn something, to engage with your life in an active and ethical way, or, if you're a writer, to write a new book! It's actually a very encouraging way of looking at things because if you think of life that way, there's no need to be afraid of making mistakes, right? Mistakes are something that you can welcome, and you should make as many as you can so that you can learn more and more and more.

RUTH OZEKI'S TIPS

▶ Procrastination is not a great strategy for coping with your perfectionism. Procrastination will prevent you from fully living your life; instead learn to appreciate your mistakes.

▶ The act of bringing anything into the world, of taking an idea and making it real, means bringing it from the state of absolute perfection in your mind into a state of relative imperfection in reality. Every novel or painting is like this: perfect in the maker's mind, but imperfectly realized. You can look at this as a mistake or simply as an opportunity to engage—because it's through the making of mistakes that we are able to live creative lives.

▶ In Japanese Zen, there are many elaborate rituals, including the tea ceremony. Everything is precise and formal and elaborate—and essentially, there is no way of performing these rituals without messing things up. You could look at the whole thing as an elaborate setup to trip people up and make them fall on their faces, but those who practice these rituals do them over and over and over again, regardless of the mistakes they make. Living life is the same. Really, living is a practice of learning to make better mistakes and to accept ourselves and our myriad imperfections. I think we need more practice in living our lives this way, especially when we're young and especially as women. It's easy for women to get caught up in trying to be perfect, so the more practice we can have making mistakes, the better. We should make many, many mistakes, and if we find ourselves being perfect all the time, we should go out of our way to put ourselves intentionally in situations where we'll screw up. Why not?

COURTNEY E. MARTIN

"I want to live in a world where people are willing to admit they are wrong in public. Some people change their viewpoint on an issue or a situation because they realize that they were wrong in their assessment of something—and that should be celebrated instead of being viewed as a weakness."

In her compelling talk for TEDx Women, Courtney E. Martin describes feeling overwhelmed by her desire to make the world a better place, wondering how people both acknowledge the reality of society's problems *and* sustain the energy to effect change. Her questions led to the beautiful book *Do It Anyway: The New Generation of Activists*, in which she profiles eight young people doing social justice work.

Martin is a writer and cultural critic who works at the nexus of journalism and activism. She is part of the OpEd Project, helping to get the voices of women and people of color onto the op-ed pages of major media sources; she was one of the founding editors of the blog *Feministing*; and she has now partnered with a colleague to develop Valenti Martin Media, a communications consulting firm focused on helping social justice organizations to increase effectiveness.

She's written several books, including *Perfect Girls, Starving Daughters: How the Quest for Perfection Is Harming Young Women*, which received a Books for a Better Life nomination and was called "smart and spirited" by the *New York Times*. She has been called "one of our most insightful culture critics and one of our finest young writers" by Parker Palmer. Her writing has been described as "varied, transformational, and necessary for us all" (Jane Fonda) and as "a hardcover punch in the gut" (Arianna Huffington). Courtney Martin studied political science and sociology at Barnard College and received a master of arts in writing and social change from the Gallatin School at New York University.

Lessons I've Learned

Be open to learning in public.

I don't remember a time when I wasn't writing online. The beginning of my freelance life, when I graduated from Barnard in 2002, coincided with the rising popularity of the Internet. It was hard to pitch a story and get it printed in a real magazine but easier to pitch to these wacky new online spaces.

I started blogging at *Feministing* in 2006. Three years into that gig, I wrote a post about chivalry, trying to unpack what it means to be a feminist in romantic relationships. I liked when guys opened doors for me but wondered if that fed a stereotype that women were weak and needed to be taken care of by men. I thought about it and felt good about the distinction that I came up with—door opening as a loving gesture versus door opening with an "I don't think you can open this *heavy* door by your little self!" attitude. What I ended up writing was that it's romantic if it happens out of care and interdependence but *not* romantic if the guy thinks you are an "invalid"—a word I was trying to use ironically.

Then the blogosphere exploded. Very quickly, the disability rights community online held me accountable for that language, saying that the word "invalid" was derogatory. A well-known blogger wrote a letter that was cosigned by nearly forty other bloggers, and there was a quickly organized online campaign to boycott *Feministing*. I remember when the shit hit the fan, sitting at my little desk in my apartment in Brooklyn by myself, feeling this sucker punch of shame. The backlash assumed I was a person who just didn't care, and I felt so misunderstood. I wanted to scream back at the computer, "I had no idea!"

I went for a walk in Prospect Park, which is what I often do when I need to gain perspective, and then I called friends who were fellow bloggers. Miriam Pérez, another *Feministing* writer, was compassionate and particularly helpful: "I know who you are and I know you didn't mean to offend people or make people feel bad," she said. "So let's think together how we can respond to this group of people." It was so helpful to have that reality check from friends who said, "You did use an offensive *word*, but you're not a terrible *person*." They could be honest while reminding me that my essence was good.

We had an online convening, during which we talked with people in the disability community about what they thought that *Feministing*—and I in particular—wasn't "getting" about disability rights. On the surface, it was a failure.

"I would love to learn more about disability studies," I said. "Are there particular readings or films or other content that you would suggest?"

Someone responded, "That's a classic privileged question. You think it's our job to educate you, to do the labor of curating some list for you."

It seemed like the people accusing us of ableism thought the convening was a PR move, and I couldn't convince them otherwise. Even so, Feministing.com took their feedback to heart and made a bunch of changes. We issued an official apology to our readers for having used words like "lame" (a derogatory word for a person unable to walk on both legs) and "crazy" (a mean way to describe someone with a mental illness). We told our readers that we would somehow find a way to include transcriptions with videos and enlisted them to help with the time-consuming work of transcribing. (None of us were getting paid.)

I would be lying if I said the whole situation didn't freak me out a little bit. It felt like my voice had a lot of power, and I was scared of that—mostly, because I didn't want to offend people. But I also felt good about having pushed through the feeling of wanting to crawl under the bed and never come out. I now knew myself to be someone who admitted when I screwed up and who cared when I hurt people. I was willing to look stupid and have difficult conversations and do all these things that are just hard for human beings. I knew that I had integrity.

You risk hurting people by telling their stories publicly, so do it responsibly.

At the same time that I was blogging for *Feministing*, I was also working on my first book, *Perfect Girls, Starving Daughters*. It had come about in a strange way, because after college I never wanted to think about body image again. I'd been around so many young women who were anxious about their bodies that I'd actually hidden the mirrors in my apartment to keep myself from being a perfectionist about my own body. Unfortunately, I couldn't avoid what was really a pervasive, wide-reaching problem, affecting people close to me. A thirteen-year-old whom I mentored told me that bagels were "evil" because they made you fat; a close friend revealed to me that she had been struggling with bulimia.

One day when I was in the YMCA, I sat in the sauna with a bunch of naked older women and just had the sense that *they* felt completely fine about their bodies. I wrote an essay about the contrast between those women and the young people around me and sent it to an anthology where it was accepted. I felt like I was done—I could really put the issue down.

Then a literary agent contacted me.

"I think you have something really important to say about this issue," she said.

"No, I really don't," I told her.

"Writers are supposed to write what they know," she responded, "and it sounds like this is something you know."

Of course, it was exciting to have attention from an agent, and I began to see that I actually did have a lot to say about women's relationships to their bodies.

In researching and writing that first book, I was aware of the volatility of "body image" as an issue and also aware of wanting to report my story ethically and accurately. It was right around the time that an author named James Frey published a memoir, *A Million Little Pieces*, which turned out to be filled with falsehoods, igniting a huge controversy. I didn't want that to happen to me, so I took careful notes to keep track of my sources, did my own fact-checking, and asked each person I interviewed to carefully review and sign a release form showing she'd agreed to be in the book.

Only after the book was published did I see the unintended side effects of my writing. Young women I'd interviewed would call or e-mail me and say, "You are not going to believe the reaction my mom had." And many of the reactions were *not good*.

In one particular instance, there was a young woman

who'd agreed to be interviewed. I made sure that she was over eighteen and asked her to sign a release; these are important steps to reporting in an ethical way. Much later, after the book was published, I learned that her mother read the interview and felt publicly shamed. She hadn't known that her daughter was talking to me, and she didn't want their family's story in every Barnes & Noble. This was, in turn, upsetting to the daughter. Of course, it had been the young woman's choice to tell her story; there was no legal obligation for her to ask her parents. But the experience made me see that storytelling is powerful and can hurt like hell in unpredictable ways.

When I wrote my next book, *Do It Anyway*, which contained in-depth profiles of young activists, I promised the interview subjects that I'd show them what was going into the book. If there was something that they couldn't stand the thought of people knowing, then I would take it out. If we got to a point when I needed to take so much out that it wouldn't be an accurate portrayal, then they just wouldn't be in the book. There was indeed one person I profiled who ended up wanting me to cut parts of the profile in a way that really changed it, and I decided that it would be better just not to include it at all. Even though it was a huge loss of time because of all the reporting and writing I'd done, it was a good way to deal with an unresolvable difference of perspective. After what had happened with *Perfect Girls*, I just didn't want to publish a book that would expose people in ways that they didn't want to be exposed.

These stories are about realizing the power of my voice and the power of my writing, and wrestling with what that power means. If you are going to be someone who believes you should take up space and put stories out in the world, you have to be mindful of the power of that. Sometimes writing my own stories and telling other people's still scares me. What keeps me going is knowing that powerful stories can lead to transformation for both the reader and the writer. When there are risks involved in doing the work that you do, it's important to connect to what's most meaningful to you about that work—to understand why you do it in the first place.

COURTNEY E. MARTIN'S TIPS

- ▶ It's important to have a community of colleagues—whether at work, outside of work, or both—that holds you accountable and is honest but also reminds you of your goodness in moments when you're feeling like a failure.

- ▶ If you're going to write about difficult subjects, you're probably going to hurt some people in the process. The question is, then: how much of that can you stand? And in what ways can you be intentional about co-creating with and preparing people? It's important to consider these questions before diving in, to equip yourself emotionally.

J. COURTNEY SULLIVAN

"As far as I'm concerned, a work of fiction is never actually finished, even after they've slapped a cover on it and put it on the shelves at Barnes and Noble. But in a way, I think the imperfections are what keep me going. There is always another chance to get it right, to say it more clearly next time."

J. Courtney Sullivan is a "born storyteller," said *Entertainment Weekly* in its review of her most recent book, *The Engagements*. The *Chicago Tribune* added, "Sullivan brilliantly captures how the vicissitudes of life—grief, infidelity, pressure—echo throughout a marriage." Sullivan's three novels, *Commencement, Maine*, and—most recently—*The Engagements*, tell stories that weave together events over time, sometimes across generations. Somehow she manages to write books that are fun to read and hard to put down but that also gracefully challenge the reader's expectations, inviting us to think in new ways about the politics of gender and class.

In person, Sullivan is lovely, charming, and funny; her low-key manner puts you completely at ease and you can almost forget that she was a bestselling author before the age of thirty. Despite a rigorous writing schedule, she never fails to make time for undergraduate students here at Smith, where she is an alumna. Last year, although she was working on a tight deadline, she agreed to Skype with a brand-new group of first-year students and answer questions about writing. We sat in a sunny classroom around a big wooden table that faced a screen, and suddenly there was Sullivan at her desk in her Brooklyn bedroom, smiling and telling the group about her own first days of college, including a teary good-bye with her parents.

Lessons I've Learned

Sometimes you have to make it up as you go along.

During college, my life consisted mostly of reading novels while wearing pajama pants. I aspired to someday write novels while wearing pajama pants, too, and for the past four years, that's more or less what I've done (with a lot of book tour travel, research, and actual clothing mixed in). But between getting my diploma and quitting my day job to write full-time, I worked as an assistant for six years—first at *Allure* magazine and later at the *New York Times*. In both places, I started as a fish out of water and had to learn on the job.

I was raised by parents who loved theater, music, art, and literature. They subscribed to the *New Yorker*, but our dinner table conversations were mostly about family gossip and what happened at school that day. We weren't intellectuals. I never really knew there *was* such a thing until I arrived in New York at the age of twenty. As I made friends, went to cocktail parties, and talked to people at work, I slowly realized that there was a whole vocabulary I didn't speak, well-known figures I didn't know, and important books I was supposed to have read but hadn't. For a long time, I played catch-up: I'd nod my head in agreement as someone detailed something they'd heard on NPR, then sneak off to the bathroom to Google what the heck they were talking about.

My entrée into publishing began somewhat inauspiciously. The first stop on my job search was a career fair at a big hotel in Times Square. In one ballroom, publishing houses were interviewing candidates. In the other, law firms were conducting interviews. My best friend from college was there with me— she wanted to work at a law firm. We waited around for what seemed like hours. She was having trouble with her boyfriend, and we were in the middle of a big discussion over what she should do about it—when suddenly, someone was yelling my name. I hadn't realized that I was up next.

I ran into the ballroom. I was not really in the right headspace for an interview, but I wasn't nervous because I had grown up surrounded by books: they were on every shelf of my house; they filled the trunk of my father's car; they came spilling out of my bedroom closet whenever I opened the door. I felt as if I had done nothing but read for the previous two decades. I had this in the bag.

To kick off the interview, the nice lady from human resources threw me a softball, asking, what were some of my favorite books? I went completely blank. I could not think of a single title. My answer was something Sarah Palin–esque, like, "My favorite books? Oh, gosh, all of them." (Even now, ten years later, I cringe over this one. Walking down the streets of Brooklyn, I'll suddenly think to myself *Bleak House*! Why didn't you say *Bleak House*? Or Willa freaking Cather, you idiot. How could you forget about her?)

Needless to say, I didn't get the job.

Eventually, though, I was hired by Condé Nast, the large magazine publisher that produces *Allure*, *Vogue*, the *New Yorker*, and *GQ*, among many others. My job was to be a "rover," basically a floating temp and the most bottom-of-the-totem-pole person at the company. As a rover, you went from one magazine to another and were at the whim of whoever hired you that week. When I worked at *House and Garden*, they let me go on photo shoots and were generally wonderful to me. But at a men's fashion magazine (that has since folded), I had to stand in a room with an enormous pile of clothing on the floor, putting it into garment bags and hanging each piece up one by one. I did that every day, eight hours a day, for two weeks. At another magazine, the women I worked for never even bothered to learn my name. They just called me "the rover." They would say things to each other like, "Oh, Jennifer, can I borrow the rover?" as if I were a vacuum cleaner. But I got the impression that as long as I didn't burn down the building I'd end up with a job, and so I kept going. And that's how I became an assistant at *Allure*.

At *Allure*, just as I had done at countless cocktail parties when I first arrived in New York, I gave myself a crash course in a new language without letting on that I was doing so. *(Bobbi Brown was a makeup artist? I thought he was a member of a boy band.)* I spent two years there. To this day, I still have no idea how to put on eyeliner, but I learned how to write about it. I wrote about makeup and celebrities almost in the way that I would write fiction—in the voice of a character. It wasn't that I desperately cared about the newest lip gloss, but the person in whose voice I was writing *did*. Once I figured that out, I was able to do it.

As an assistant, I worked crazy hours, helping two high-powered editors and all their writers—I'd be at the office until seven p.m. and then I'd go home and keep working. It was really fast paced. But it was also wonderful, because they actually let me write. I did a column called Total Makeover, in the Features section, and one day, I saw a woman reading it at the Laundromat and could not believe it: I had written this thing and she was reading it. It was the coolest feeling. I had always written for fun, but at *Allure* I learned how to be a professional: how to take edits; how to write to space and to a deadline. And I met so many amazing writers and editors who I know to this day. It was a real education.

There were certain unspoken rules at Condé Nast that surprised me. I had interned at the *Atlantic Monthly* during college and I had worked in other offices, but I had never been in an environment where the social guidelines were so proscribed that it was almost like being in a Victorian novel: "You can't speak to this person unless spoken to," or "You can't ride the elevator with that person," or "You never walk into this person's office without permission." At the time, one of my best friends from college was working for this really scary attorney, and we both would—on occasion—cry in the bathroom stall and then e-mail each other about what was happening in our workplaces.

Meanwhile, on weekends, I was working away on my first novel, *Commencement*. A famous bestselling novelist wrote an essay for *Allure*, and when I interviewed her for our Contributors page, she said she was home "writing and waiting for the washing machine repairman." This is not exactly the most glamorous statement, but I held it with me for years: the thought that as someone who made her living writing novels, you could be home on a Tuesday afternoon *writing and waiting for the washing machine repairman*.

I left *Allure* when I got the opportunity to work as a research assistant for a *New York Times* columnist. I loved the job. I immersed myself in my work and learned tons about world politics. I already read the *New York Times* and had a pretty good sense of what was happening in the news, but now I was working for an op-ed columnist who was covering Iraq and Afghanistan, women's issues, workers' rights, and poverty. I got to meet heads of state and amazing activists and thinkers, but sometimes I had to figure things out as I went. I couldn't just stop in the middle of a deadline to say, "Excuse me, what is 'yellow cake' and why is it a problem? To me it sounds delicious." (Yellowcake—one word—turns out to be a radioactive powder made from uranium.)

One day, I got a phone call from someone who asked if my boss wanted to take a meeting with POTUS the following morning. I had no idea what POTUS meant, so I nearly said, no, thanks. Luckily, I ran it by my boss first. "Do you want to meet with POTUS?" I asked in a bored tone, as if I could anticipate him saying no. Instead, he said, "Of course!" in such a way that I suddenly realized where I'd seen the acronym before. POTUS meant "President of the United States."

Throughout my time at *Allure* and the *New York Times*, I continued writing my first novel and eventually I published it. When I sold my second novel, *Maine*, I left the *Times*. I could finally support myself as a novelist. I could stay home on a Tuesday writing and waiting for the washing machine repairman. I've learned that every professional opportunity is something you should seize upon—you never know where it might lead you. And that if you have a passion, it might have to be a hobby for a long time before it becomes a job. That's okay. Keep going, work hard, and don't be afraid to figure it out as you go along.

J. COURTNEY SULLIVAN'S TIPS

▶ Always say yes to new opportunities. Throughout my twenties, I had a rule for myself: if someone asked me to write an article, I said yes no matter what. That led me to go outside of my comfort zone, to build up a great resume, and to make tons of contacts.

▶ Today's assistants are tomorrow's head honchos. After ten years in New York, I've been amazed to see that my fellow former assistants are now leading the charge—one is editor in chief of a magazine; others are bestselling authors. Keep in touch with people and be a kind and generous coworker. You never know where it might lead you in the future.

CAROL S. DWECK

"As I was playing it safe and avoiding setbacks, I was mesmerized by kids in our research studies who approached really hard puzzles saying things like, 'I love a challenge!' To me, the idea of potential failure was unacceptable—but they were rolling up their sleeves and trying to get something out of this. If ever there were role models for me, it was these ten-year-old children saying, 'Bring it on!'"

Dr. Carol S. Dweck doesn't use the word "smart" to describe people—ever. When I prompted her to talk about one of her graduate school professors by asking, "So you thought he was really smart?" she playfully countered, "I never used that word!"

There was a time when educators and psychologists thought that your IQ determined what you were capable of—but that was before Carol Dweck came on the scene and began publishing her research. Dweck, a Stanford University professor, is one of the world's leading researchers on motivation. Her research focuses on why people succeed and how to help them succeed. She says, "My work has shown that people's mindsets about their abilities (whether they see them as fixed traits or as qualities that can be developed) can have a profound impact. Those who believe their intelligence and talents can be developed take on more challenges, bounce back from setbacks, and often achieve more—and when people are taught this 'growth mindset' their resilience and achievement are boosted." Educators see evidence of this when Dweck's ideas are integrated into their practice. For example, Project Coach, an out-of-school program developed by Smith College for youth in Springfield, Massachusetts, teaches at-risk teenagers to be sport coaches for kids. The teens come in with below-average GPAs and learn about growth mindset as a guiding philosophy to use in their coaching and their own lives. "If they believe, 'I'm just not good at school,'" says director Kayleigh Colombero, "they won't improve." The project explicitly encourages a growth mindset, using athletes and coaches to teach kids that practice and dedication lead to an increase in talent. Kids' GPAs increase *a full point* on average during their year of being mentored through the project.

In addition to teaching at Stanford, Dweck has held professorships at Columbia and Harvard; has lectured to business, sports, and education groups all over the world; has won numerous awards; and has been elected to the American Academy of Arts and Sciences and to the National Academy of Sciences. Her work has been featured in publications like the *New Yorker, Time, Newsweek,* the *New York Times,* the *Wall Street Journal,* and the *Washington Post* and she has appeared on *Today, Good Morning America, 20/20,* and NPR's *Morning Edition.* Her widely acclaimed book *Mindset* has been translated into over twenty languages.

Lessons I've Learned

Don't let the need to be seen as perfect by those you admire keep you from developing mentoring relationships.

I was the best speller in my grade school, and my teachers wanted to send me to a districtwide contest, but I refused. In middle school, I was the star French pupil, and the principal asked if I would compete in a citywide competition, but I said no. Being at the top of my class was my claim to fame, and I worried about what would become of my status if I failed.

Many years later, when I was a graduate student in psychology at Yale, the need to uphold my image as "smart" was still, in some ways, holding me back. It was the late 1960s and, like other young people, I wanted to change the world. I began taking classes with a professor named Seymour Sarason, who was unusual in our field at that time because he was interested in applying his research to the real-life problems of children's learning and educational change. I took several courses with him and deeply admired his important work and his wisdom.

Then one day, I was sitting in my adviser's office and he reported to me that he'd had a conversation with Sarason, who apparently thought I was "really, really smart." It felt great! I was thrilled, just basking in the approval and respect.

But for the rest of my graduate career, I steered clear of Seymour Sarason. Why? Because I had the validation I craved.

Because in my desire for perfection, I thought, "What if I interact more with him and don't say brilliant things? Then I might no longer have his blessing." Looking back, I think it was a shame, because he was working on so many things that interested me. Instead of asking about his ideas and sharing mine, I robbed myself of the opportunity to be mentored by someone I greatly admired.

The irony is that in my research, I was starting to look at how people cope with failure. I was asking what allows some children to cope well and causes others to act as though a failure is the end of the world. I hadn't yet realized that this work was "me-search"—research that was compelling because of my own experiences and issues. I had never really failed, but when you're a person who wants to be perfect, who wants to be validated, the specter of failure is always there.

Developing a "growth mindset" can sustain you when you're taking risks in your career.

My ideas had grown out of research on learned helplessness, which demonstrated that when animals were exposed to shocks which they couldn't escape, they eventually gave up trying to— even after those shocks *became* escapable. The animals learned that their behavior had no impact on their environment. I thought there were important analogs with people: my theory was that when some children worked on tasks and failed, it made them stop believing in their abilities—and so they stopped trying.

In order to learn more, I was doing studies in which I gave fifth graders different kinds of problems, puzzles that we could make easier or more difficult. When some kids got puzzles that they couldn't solve, they stopped working and said, "I can't do this." They thought the failure meant they had no talent, and they became helpless or incapacitated. Others said things like, "This is my favorite kind of test!" They actually revved up their energy and taught themselves new ways of approaching the problems, sometimes even solving problems that were supposedly too hard for them. Difficulty motivated them, which actually caused them to *increase* their abilities.

So I wondered: why did some kids see failure as meaning that they lacked ability, but others saw it as an exciting opportunity to learn? The children we studied were equally capable, but some just wanted to validate their abilities through solving the puzzles correctly, while others wanted to grow or increase their abilities through trying. Maybe, my students and I thought, "ability" itself had different meanings to them. Those who just wanted to validate it were seeing it as a fixed thing—you show your ability to the world through your performance, and the world passes judgment, telling you whether it's high or low. But those who wanted to grow their ability saw it as much more dynamic, as something that could be developed.

Before starting on this new line of thinking, I had been part of a group of psychologists around the world who studied people's "attributions" (explanations) for their success and failure, and my research was successful and well received. As I developed these new theories and questions about the meaning of ability, I was suddenly stepping out of that nice, safe group of peer researchers—essentially venturing into unknown territory to do something new. Furthermore, my work was going to challenge the received wisdom of the time, which was that ability is static. I knew that it might not be well accepted and that I was exposing myself to the possibility of failure for the first time.

Everything was at stake. I knew that I wouldn't be able to easily publish this research—it was too new—which made me worry for the graduate students who were devoted to these ideas but needed to publish in order to get jobs. At the same time, I believed in my work and knew that in order to grow—both professionally and personally—I would have to pursue it.

I remember talking to a colleague who was also developing ideas that were new and radical in the field of psychology, and she told me that she was so anxious that one day, she was sure she had cancer; the next day, she thought she was going to have a heart attack. There was just this feeling that you were putting yourself in danger. But it's always reassuring to hear that someone you respect is going through something similar and to be reminded that this is part of the creative process.

It was also helpful that as my research began spelling out the characteristics of the fixed mindset versus the growth mindset, I began to see the ways in which these insights could apply to me. In a fixed mindset, you value looking smart over learning. You think effort is bad because if you have a high ability, then you shouldn't need to make a lot of effort. You think that failures define you. In the growth mindset, you value learning and effort, and you see mistakes and setbacks as tools for learning. So these discoveries were almost like a road map that I could use in forging ahead. If I heard myself thinking, "Oh, this is hard. I don't really want to do it," I'd go, "No, no, no, no, no! You have to do it."

I taught myself to work toward having a growth mindset by listening for moments when my own "fixed mindset" revealed itself. One night when I was driving by the psychology building, I saw lights on in faculty offices. "Why are they working at eleven p.m.?" I wondered. "They must not be as smart as I am." But then I recognized this as a "fixed mindset" thought and said to myself, "Maybe they have new data that they're excited about. Maybe they're working on something really passionately."

My nascent growth mindset was really put to the test when our work on mindsets was initially turned down by the top psychology journals. When you're doing something new and the editor and peer reviewers aren't familiar with it, it can take longer than usual to publish. But with every rejection I said, "Okay, what do I learn from this? How do I make it better?" And even though the research wasn't immediately hailed in print, I began presenting talks about it and could see that people related to it both on an intellectual, theoretical level and on a personal level. Everyone wanted to talk about it, to understand it.

Over time, our research became internationally recognized; my students and I have received numerous honors and awards, and the ideas that we developed about mindsets are becoming integral to the way in which people understand learning. I'm very fortunate that I was able to tune in to my own findings, to understand that I needed to develop a growth mindset in order to take risks and do my best work. If you choose to learn more about the concepts of "fixed mindset" versus "growth mindset"—whether through my book or online—I hope that these ideas will be helpful for you, too.

CAROL S. DWECK'S TIPS

▶ My sixth-grade teacher seated us around our classroom room in IQ order. I grew up feeling like I could never let my guard down because I had to uphold the image of being "smart" all the time. Many years later, letting go of this allowed me to take the risks that were essential to growing both personally and professionally. I've learned that in order to develop into the people we want to become, we need to let go of our need for continual validation.

▶ Understand that even though change isn't always easy, each of us has the capacity to develop a "growth mindset" approach to our lives. When you have a "growth mindset," you understand that mistakes and setbacks are an inevitable part of learning.

Acknowledgments

I'd like to thank the brilliant and brave contributors for the time they devoted to speaking with me and for their generosity in telling their stories. I'm also grateful to Lindsay Edgecombe, my agent, who immediately "got" this book and has been helpful in so many ways—by setting a deadline for me to complete the proposal, providing lots of useful feedback, and finding a fabulous editor. Kate Napolitano, my editor at Plume, has been a wise and motivating force throughout the entire process.

This book was inspired by conversations with Smith College's Maureen A. Mahoney and Jennifer L. Walters. Their interest in women's narratives and their mentorship of me has been life-changing. I'd like to thank Sue Briggs, too, for conversations we have had as part of the Women's Narratives Project. Ally Einbinder is an extraordinary person and incredible colleague. Her creative work, making music as part of the excellent band Potty Mouth, is an ongoing inspiration.

I appreciate the colleagues and friends who took time to help me think about and connect with potential contributors: Patsy Barber, Emily Berkman, Ellen Carter, Liz Garbus, Jessica Goldstein, Rachel Hass, Tracy Kramer, Iris Newalu, Jessica Nicoll, Fran Rosenfeld, and Rachel Simmons. I want to thank friends who read drafts and gave me useful input: Heather Abel, Joe Bacal, Arielle Eckstut, Lisa Papademetriou, and Laura Sedlock.

My parents, Jim and Joan Levine, are always supportive; this past year, they offered ideas *and* child care in order to help me get to the finish line. Thank you also to Josh, Debby, Joel, and Gabrielle for cheering me along the way.

Finally, I'd like to thank my son, Elijah, for his enthusiasm about this book. Elijah, you wanted me to write about the mistake of leaving the ice cream in the microwave for too many seconds so that it melted instead of just softening—and now I have! I'd like to thank my daughter, Edie, who led by example, often busy with her own "wert." And I'd like to thank Joe Bacal, who makes everything more fun.